Enjoy my wanderings
Thanks for the purchase.

Tom Laughlin

The Summer of '71

Hitchhiking to Maturity

by

Tom Laughlin

The Summer of '71

Hitchhiking to Maturity

Published by

splatteredinkpress.com

ISBN 978-1-939294-21-0

"Two roads diverged in a wood, and I -
I took the one less traveled by,
And that has made all the difference."
Robert Frost "The Road Not Taken"

<u>Dedicated to</u>
H. Reed & Robie Laughlin
My models of love, family, and parenthood.
They taught me to take the road less traveled.

"You are the wind beneath my wings..."

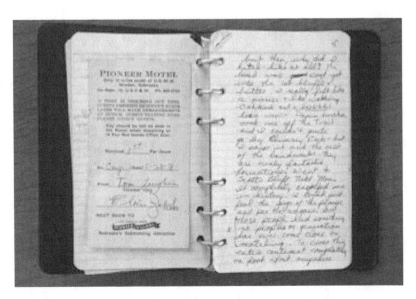

The Journal today

Acknowledgments

This book has been formulating in my mind for over forty years, but it never would have been written without the encouragement and support of a number of good friends and family.

In particular I need to thank Scott Christian, C.E. Sikkenga, Jim O'Neill, Tom Gillem, John Kropf, and Rebecca Romine for reading my first drafts and encouraging me to forge on and continue writing. Scott and C.E. helped with grammar and edited early drafts. Tom Gillem offered valuable expertise and experienced opinions. Lydia Stewart Waring Meyers provided me with a thorough and helpful edit as I neared the end, and family members helped me remember events and gave organizational changes. Of course I need to thank Tricia McDonald of Splattered Ink Press for her coaching, editing, and encouragement.

And finally, I must acknowledge my parents, friends, and all the drivers who picked me up along the way and made this entire experience the wonderful memory that it is. Thank you.

Table of Contents

The Journal - 2011

"Hey Dad, what's this?"

It was the spring of 2011. I was searching through the basement collection of old books and family memorabilia with my two sons, Matt and Andy.

Matt was holding a shoe box labeled "The Summer of '71" in black marker. Inside were maps, letters, tourist flyers, some old ticket stubs, and about twenty grainy snapshots. As we looked through it I said, "Wow – I forgot I still had that stuff. Is the journal there?"

"Is this what you mean?" Andy asked as he held up a small black notebook. "What is all this?"

"It's a journal I kept back in 1971. That summer I hitchhiked to San Francisco, then to ROTC Boot camp at Fort Lewis, Washington, and finally spent a month in Europe. I kept this journal of my thoughts and observations along the way. Geez - That's been forty years," I said as I leafed through the pages. "It was a great trip and played a huge part in my growing up. Look at this stuff. I need to sit down and reread this. Maybe I'll put it in the computer and share it with you guys."

"Yeah – We'd like that. Let us read it when you're done."

As I read the journal and typed it for my family, I realized many things had changed, and many had stayed the same, in the forty years since I took the trip. As a retired high school history teacher, I also realized many historical events and cultural changes had taken place in the world since then. The journal told of a young man's experiences, but it also described many subtle changes in history. It had become an historical document.

In 1971 I was twenty-one and a junior at the University of Michigan. I was adventurous, curious, and wanted to travel. And just as I was growing and changing and learning, our nation was at a turning point. 1971 was a year without any great defining moments, but still with historical significance. It was a year of contrasts - the conservative, idealistic vision of the 1950s and early 1960s had not disappeared, but the rash extremes of the Sixties Counterculture were also starting to become an established part of American society.

Richard Nixon was in his third year as President and Watergate was over a year away. The Vietnam War had been going on for over six years and the split of pro and anti-war supporters was getting wider as the

Pentagon Papers were released and Vietnam Veterans Against the War began to testify in Congress. There were still approximately 200,000 Americans in the jungles of Southeast Asia with no apparent end to the fighting. The Cold War with the Soviet Union seemed to be a non-stop competition of one-upmanship as both nations put men into space. The U.S. sent two expeditions to the moon, while the U.S.S.R. launched the first orbital space station. Domestic policy was also heavily influenced by attitudes towards the war and the competition with the communists.

The Youth Counterculture of the late Sixties was very much in vogue. Hippies, Yippies, sex, drugs, rock and roll, and the Generation Gap were all very common and were becoming readily accepted parts of the American lifestyle by 1971. While many television shows like *Mayberry R.F.D., The Carol Burnett Show,* and *Here's Lucy* still reflected the all-American ideal of the 1950's, there were also more socially controversial shows starting to appear, such as *All in the Family,* and *The Mary Tyler Moore Show.* Music also reflected the divergent direction of society with music by James Taylor, The Partridge Family, John Denver, Smokey Robinson, and The Carpenters hitting the top of the charts along with counterculture, anti-war groups like The Rolling Stones, John Lennon, Joan Baez, and Bob Dylan. That great diversity of political, social, and cultural ideas reflected the year of 1971.

This is a story of a young man coming to maturity, but it is also a reflection of the times in the late 1960's and the early 1970's. I took a journey that changed my life while giving me a great perspective to view the United States and our nation's role in the world. From the end of May to the end of August I hitchhiked from Michigan to California, then north to Fort Lewis, Washington. After six weeks of military training at Fort Lewis, I spent the month of August traveling in Europe. I traveled alone, but gained new friends every day. This is the story of that summer adventure.

Thousands of young people have journeyed through the United States and Europe either during, or right after, their college years. Many of them went more miles and spent more time on the road than I did, but in many ways our experiences were very similar. Over the past forty years I have met many fellow travelers and we have shared fond memories of travel and adventure. But I believe my combination of hitchhiking in the United States and Europe in one summer provided a unique situation and offered a different perspective on things. Hopefully this memoir is a reminder of the accomplishments and experiences of my fellow travelers. May the ramblings of my summer trip bring back pleasant memories to them.

During the trip, I tried to keep my journal up to date, sometimes writing two or three times a day. Usually I would make an entry in the evening recapping the day's happenings. But sometimes I was not as diligent and did not make an entry for a couple of days, at which point I would try to catch up with where I had been and what I had seen. This was especially true

during my travels through Europe, where I was frequently distracted by the culture and excitement of
being in a foreign land. The entries sometimes jump
around, as my thoughts went from impression to
impression.

Somehow I managed to keep that little notebook for
forty years. The journal has become the basis of this
book and for my observations about society, history,
and me. I will copy the journal in its entirety, and
explain the entries as I go. As much as possible I will
keep the spelling and punctuation intact, only making
some minimal editing and corrections to help with
readership and understanding. The pictures included
were taken with a small Kodak Instamatic camera and
are as grainy and simplistic as would seem appropriate
for forty year old snapshots.

The pictures and thoughts of the journal are those
of a twenty-one year old who had traveled before, but in
many ways was just seeing the world for the first time.
The reflections on my fellow man, on nature, and on
society are often quick, gut reactions, but are observations that have stayed with me my whole life. Over the
years I have learned to appreciate how special that time
was to me, and the nation. I look at the world around
me today and think back to the simplicity of that time
and realize how much was learned. It was a summer of
discovery, a summer of adventure, and a summer of
growth. Most of all it was the summer when I learned
who I was.

Joe the Trucker

To Ma, Who Worried!

I was at the toll plaza at the junction of I-80 and I-294, outside Chicago, when the eighteen-wheeler slowed to a stop.

"Climb in quick. The cops don't like it if I stop here!" the burly driver yelled out the window.

I climbed into the big rig and threw my backpack and duffle bag behind the seat as the driver shifted into gear and started down the road.

"Where ya headed?" he asked.

"Thanks for stopping. Just heading west. Eventually I plan to end up at my aunt's in San Francisco."

He was a Vietnam vet named Joe - which sounded like he could be anyone, and in a sense he did seem to represent an average Joe. Short, stocky, strong arms, and a round face with a growth of stubble on his chin, he fit my stereotype of a long-distance truck driver. He was in his late twenties, spent two weeks at a time on the road and had very little home life.

"This truck is my home for right now." he said. He wasn't married and figured he wouldn't be until he stopped driving, but that did not seem to bother him. "I've got plenty of girlfriends here on the road. I meet up with them as I travel." and he patted his CB radio as an indication of how he stayed in touch with anyone that meant anything to him. "So what's your deal? Where'd ya come from?"

"Started this morning in Ann Arbor, Michigan. I've been getting pretty lucky with rides. But most have only been for ten to twenty miles. I think I've had ten different rides up to this point."

"Well, you can go as long as you want with me; I'm going to the west coast."

"I won't be staying all the way to the west coast. I'm in no hurry, so I'll get out later this evening. I just want to see some of the country – I'll probably take five or six days to get there. But I do appreciate the offer."

"Hey, no problem. Just let me know when you want out. How long are you planning on staying in San Francisco?" Joe asked.

"Well – that takes a bit of explanation." I said. "I'm on my way to Fort Lewis, Washington. I'm in ROTC at the University of Michigan and I have to attend summer camp for six weeks. So my aunt's house is just a stop-over before I thumb up the coast to Fort Lewis."

"Okay – that puts a different twist on all this. Tell me more."

So, as we rumbled down the road, I proceeded to give Joe a little background.

"I graduated from high school in 1968. I have two older brothers and they both went to Vietnam. I've heard about their experiences. I figured I would probably get drafted after college and I'd rather be an officer in the army. I guess I felt I should do my patriotic duty, too. I still hadn't formed a definitive opinion about Vietnam, but it seemed the right thing to do. Consequently, I applied for, and was offered, a ROTC scholarship. You know about the Reserve Officer Training Corps don't you?"

"Oh sure," said Joe. "What did you get for that?"

"Well, it pays for my tuition and books and I get a monthly living allowance, so it's been a good deal, but I have a four year active duty commitment after graduation. Part of the ROTC program is the requirement to attend 'ROTC Summer Camp' - the ROTC version of Boot Camp - for six weeks in the summer of a cadet's junior year. That's the justification for this trip - to get to Fort Lewis and attend camp."

"Okay, that makes sense." Joe said. "But why go all the way to Lewis? Is that the only place they have the training?"

"No, not at all. Most of the cadets from Michigan go to Fort Riley, Kansas. But last fall the senior ROTC cadets spent a day in class giving presentations on their experiences at camp. Most of them had attended camp at Fort Riley, since that is the training installation for the Midwest region. None of the cadets had a particularly bad experience at Fort Riley, but most of them described it as hot, dusty, bug-infested, and fifty miles from anything approaching civilization."

"Yeah, I've heard that about Riley myself," said Joe, never taking his eyes off the road.

"Well, as I was absorbing that vision in my mind, a cadet whose family home was in Portland, Oregon, stepped to the podium and explained how he had gone to Fort Lewis, Washington, since it was closer to his home. Lewis - as you probably know - is just outside Tacoma, Washington, and close to lots of places I'd like to visit if I get some time off - Seattle, Olympia National Park, and the ocean, for example. As the cadet discussed his experiences I started thinking that a summer in the Northwest sounded a bit more attractive than a summer in Kansas.

"After class, I casually asked Major Radamaker, our instructor, how I could get orders to attend camp at Fort Lewis instead of Fort Riley. He said, 'If it's cheaper

for the government to send you to Lewis, they will do it.'
I asked him how that worked and he replied, 'The
government pays all your transportation expenses from
your local address to and from camp, so if they can
save money, they'll send you to Fort Lewis. Of course,
you will have to put in a special request since your
home of record is Michigan.'

"I didn't want to go to Fort Riley – Fort Lewis sounded much more interesting. It wasn't that the military
training was going to be any different at either place – it
would be Hell no matter where I went. But I knew there
would be opportunities to get off post on weekends I
could get a chance to see the surrounding countryside.
All I had to do was figure out a way to convince the
army it would be better to send me to Fort Lewis.

"By the time I had to fill out the paperwork a couple
of weeks later, I had come up with a plan which seemed
simple. My mother's younger sister, Becky, lives in San
Francisco and she always said I'm welcome to visit. So
when I filled out the request for orders I explained I
would be in San Francisco prior to attending camp and
it would be cheaper for the army to send me to Fort
Lewis. I'm sure the explanation of how the army could
save money was the clinching factor, and in about six
weeks my orders came back authorizing me to attend
camp at Fort Lewis.

"As I was waiting for my orders, I started looking at
the dates of camp and planning the rest of the summer.
ROTC camp was going to be in the middle of the sum-

mer - from mid-June to the end of July - so it would be impractical to get a job. I had worked at a local factory the previous two summers, but I knew they wouldn't rehire me for only a couple of weeks. There was time before and after camp - school got out in May and fall term starts in September. So why not travel? I want to see the West Coast, go to Europe to visit my Swedish friend Thomas, and see some of the places I had been reading about. This seemed to be the perfect time. I can go to Aunt Becky's, experience the West, go to camp in July, and then travel to Europe. It all seems pretty simple."

"Okay, it does seem to make sense, but why didn't you just let Uncle Sam pay for the trip to your aunt's?" Joe asked.

"I probably could have, but I had time and I wanted to see things like this," and I waved my hand as we passed a cornfield in western Illinois. "Besides, I wanted to save as much of my army pay as possible. Hitchhiking to San Francisco seemed like a good solution to me. Of course, I still had to convince my parents it would work. Naturally, they had some concerns, but I was confident I could talk them into letting me go. I have done a lot of hitchhiking in college, usually the hundred miles from Ann Arbor to Port Huron, Michigan, so I thought they would have some confidence in my ability to do this.

"I went home one weekend and talked about my plan with Mom and Dad. They are pretty good about letting me make my own decisions, but they have a way of letting me know their thoughts. My mother is the cautious one and of course was worried about my safety and well being.

"She said stuff like, 'You're going to be all alone! You're not going to have anyone else to be with or to protect you.'

"I explained to her that that was how I wanted it - I wanted to be alone and independent and not be tied down to a schedule.

"Mom has always had a an independent streak herself, so she finally came around to the idea when I said I would call home every night, would be exceedingly careful about rides, and even promised to break off the trip and take a bus to California if necessary."

Joe smiled. "Sounds like something I'd tell my mother," he said laughing.

"Dad was more skeptical. He weighs the options of any decision with very little conversation. He will mentally think things through, ask a few questions, and then make up his mind. When he finally explains his decision, it's usually a quiet, simple statement that gets directly to the point."

"Dad would say things like, 'Why do you want to do this'? and 'What's your plan'?"

"This was the question I had been preparing for. 'Dad - I think I'm searching for something. Not sure what it is, but I just feel a little unsettled in my life right now.'

"What are you searching for?" Dad asked. "You have things pretty well laid out for you with ROTC and school."

"I know. I think that's the problem. Everything seems too well planned right now. I'll graduate next year, then go into the army for at least four years. If I get out of the army - and I don't know about that part - I'll teach school. It all seems too carefully planned. I guess I just haven't fully accepted it. I want to travel and see the world. I want to meet different people and see different cultures. I'm just not sure where I'm going, but this summer will probably be my last opportunity to travel like this, to be independent and see what's out there. That's why I say I'm still searching."

I looked over at Joe. He was listening intently. "Dad hesitated and he got his classic look that he makes when he is trying to think of an answer. I knew he was mulling things over in his head."

"When Dad asked, 'How much will it cost?' I knew that was his way of saying it was okay."

"Not much – I think I can do it for a couple hundred dollars," was my answer. "I'm going to keep costs down as low as possible."

He'd say things like, "Where will you stay?   What will you do if..."

"Dad's questions were pretty simple, but they cut to the heart of the matter in a very unemotional, logical way.   After thinking it through he explained his decision to my mother, 'Well, I guess I can see his reasoning.   Maybe this will be the end of some of his crazy ideas.   Maybe it will help him settle down when it's all done'."

I laughed as I said that last part to Joe.   "I'm not sure about that though.   I just like to travel too much! Anyways, I started out two days ago and went to Ann Arbor with my girlfriend, Jackie.   I was supposed to leave yesterday, but it was raining and miserable, so it was easy to justify staying another day with her.   She took me to I-94 this morning and I got on my way. That's why I was standing at the toll plaza when you picked me up!"

I felt I had been monopolizing the conversation for the last twenty miles, so I asked, "You've been to 'Nam. What do you think?"

Maybe it was me, or maybe it was just the question, but the temperature in the truck seemed to rise as Joe thought about his answer.

"I was drafted, so of course I was a grunt - you know, an infantryman, a ground pounder!" Joe said, a bit red faced.   "Spent exactly 365 days in 'Nam. No more. No less. That's one of the problems over there - you aren't sent over as a group. You come in as an individual and you leave as an individual. Everyone has a 'Count Down Calendar' going from day one.

"Sometimes it wasn't too bad, but other times it was Hell. Growing up I always wanted to be a soldier, so when I was drafted I was excited and figured I was doing my part to protect our country from communism. My father fought in World War II and I figured it was the right thing to do. When I first went in, I thought I was really going to make a difference. I would go over there and kill a bunch of Gooks and save the World from Communism. But after a while I began to realize I just wanted to get out of there alive."

"You sound like you've changed your mind about the war?" I said.

Joe just looked straight ahead and drove down the interstate for another mile or so before he answered. "Oh yeah - it will change you! When I first went in, I couldn't imagine the communists taking over that place. But the more I was in country; the more I realized that it's a mess over there and we have to take some of the blame. There isn't any direction to the military plans. We win a village one day, and 'Charlie' takes it back the next night. We just seem to be spinning our wheels. Our government doesn't seem to know what they're doing. They don't want to increase the manpower in 'Nam because it will lead to more protests. They bomb the shit out of the North and nothing is accomplished. And then they try to tell us we can still win the war - but if you ask any soldier on the ground, they'll all say the same thing - What are we going to win?"

"Yeah, that's what I've heard from lots of vets. My brother, Fred, is a good example. He was a West Point graduate, went to 'Nam and had a distinguished career - medals and everything - but he got out of the army as soon as he could last year and is a member of Veterans Against the Vietnam War. Makes it confusing for someone like me. I want to do my duty, but I don't want to get into a losing cause. I guess I'm still trying to figure out where I stand on all this."

Joe's explanation seemed to be a string of contradictions about the war - but then, that was the confusing mess that was Vietnam. We talked about the pros and cons of the war. Joe was open and candid about the problems we were facing over there. It was refreshing to hear both sides explained by someone who had been there.

Around 6:00 he pulled into a truck stop and Joe insisted on buying me dinner. I was impressed with his willingness to listen to my ideas and made it a point to not eat too much and take advantage of his charity. We had a great time together.

About 8:30 in the evening, after traveling through western Illinois and eastern Iowa, I decided it was time to stop for the night. The weather was warm and the new shoots of corn in the gently rolling fields seemed a perfect place to set up camp.   After we passed a couple of nice Iowa cornfields I said to my new friend, "Joe, can you pull over? I think I want to get out right here?"

His reply, of course, was "Where? Here? There's nothing around here except a cornfield!"

"I know - that's where I'm going to camp tonight!"

So he pulled over. I had been with Joe for about six hours and we had quickly become friends. I felt like I had learned a lot from him - not just about the war, but about another lifestyle I did not know. Joe asked me again if I knew what I was doing, then dropped me off next to a beautiful cornfield with one big maple tree

Sunrise at my first campground. I wrote:
The dew on the corn is a symbol of the freshness came with a good night's rest.

about a hundred yards from the road. I got out, hopped over a little fence, waved him farewell, and settled in for the night under that lone tree. I had already decided to camp as much as possible, and this Iowa cornfield seemed appropriate for my first night. Little did I know at the time that compared to some of my future sleeping spots, this cornfield would seem like a luxury suite.

Since this trip was to be an adventure, I spent very little on camping supplies, backpacks, or any of the fancy equipment available on the market. All my gear was stuffed into a small gym bag and an even smaller Boy Scout backpack. Dad and I had carefully planned what I would need. One extra pair of jeans, a shirt, a windbreaker, and a limited number of underwear were my only clothes. There was no food or water packed, since that could be bought along the way. I also had an old army poncho. That would be my rain protection, ground-cover, and even a tent, since we had devised some small poles to be used to make the poncho into a little shelter. On top of all this was a very small, but warm, sleeping bag. However, it did not take long on the road to realize my backpack was bulky and over-stuffed, so I was constantly purging things from it as the trip progressed. The first things to go - after un-successfully trying to rig up my little tent shelter that first night - were the poles Dad had so patiently crafted.

I settled into my little campsite. My adventure had begun and I was way too excited to sleep. The tree was not beautiful, and was late in leafing out to provide any shade or protection. But it still was my shelter for the night and provided a warm welcome. I quietly sat under the tree, reflected on the day, and wrote my first journal entry. I thought about my family and who I was and what I was learning. It had been a good first day. I had traveled about 450 miles, met some interesting people, and found a perfect spot to spend the night. Things were working out.

May 26, 1971:

Didn't really start - a false start. Miserable day so not a bad idea. "Leaving makes the welcome better." (me) Started with $14.00.

May 27:

Perfect day. Got out of A2 by 9:00. Made it to Homestead, Iowa. Could have gone to Des Moines but wanted to set up camp. Great location in an Iowa cornfield. I'm a little bit jittery but I'm sure I'll sleep tonight. All most exactly 12 hrs on the road and about 500 mi covered. Couldn't get to [call the] folks, hope they're not too worried. Sorry Dad, after all that work and thought, but these ponchos look good and think I'll be great tonite. Stars are coming out and the sun has gone its way – wonder if I'll ever catch it? Lots of thoughts go through your head as you're waiting. It will take a couple of days to formulate them. One thing for sure – Don't be a truck driver! It's a G__D__ rough life and rough ride. But they roll!

There sure are some beautiful farms out here. Oh, to compare the view now to the one I saw standing on a ramp south of Gary/Chicago. 1000% difference and sooo much nicer here (cleaner).

Believe it or not, it's happening. My dream trip has really begun and there's only me and my friends now and I only see some of them for a very short time.

WOW – What can I say. I'm the luckiest guy in the world! Thanks! Thanks Mom & Dad! Thanks world! Thanks God...

Wednesday, May 26 was rainy and cool, so it was easy to rationalize staying in Ann Arbor with Jackie another day. We had been dating for over a year and had been seeing each other just about every day since the fall. Our relationship was at the point where I was trying to decide if it was going to last. I had some fear of commitment, and was not sure I was ready to settle down. But I had all summer to figure that out, so why not enjoy her company for one more night.

The next morning Jackie took me south of town to I-94, dropped me at the highway ramp and my journey began. The reference to starting with "$14.00" is an indication of how little cash I always carried. I had some traveler's checks hidden in my pack, but I never carried much cash, just in case. One of the goals of the trip was to travel as cheaply as possible, so the less cash I had, the cheaper I would be.

I planned to call home each night to report where I was. We had arranged a simple signal. I would call collect from a pay phone, asking for "Tom Laughlin". In those days, the operator (Yes – a real person!) would say something like "I have a collect call from Des Moines, Iowa, for Tom Laughlin". Mom or Dad would then say I was not home, there would be no charge, but they would know where I was. Since there obviously was not a pay phone in the middle of the cornfield, I could not call that first night. Most nights though I did call, and it seemed to be enough to satisfy the folks as to where I was and that I was safe.

I kept track of the drivers for each day in the back of my journal. Instead of listing them all on one long list at the end, I've decided to put them with each day's entries so you can see the types of rides I had when describing drivers. Some, you can see, were nameless and only took me a couple of miles. Others - like Joe the truck driver - became friends and contributed to the lessons learned on the trip.

DRIVERS - DAY 1

1. *PH – A2 = Jac – Sorry Jac!*
2. *A2 - Waterloo = "Free Lt Calley" vet, country music, good guy*
3. *To K'zoo = Cal Michels – great – teacher at EMU – Stop in!*
4. *To Benton Harbor = Salesman – nice – "Wish I could go!"*
5. *Kid = couple miles*

6. *2 Crazy girls = coined phrase and called me a "professional hitchhiker". What's that? To Michigan City*

7 – 10. Short rides past Chicago

11. *Truck driver. $100.00 fine for no permit. To Route 66 (Joliet)*

12. *To Homestead, Iowa = Joe a trucker. Away from home for 2 week plus. Bought me dinner. Told all about the Army. Good head*

Wanderlust

It was a tumultuous time in American history. There was an unpopular war being fought overseas. Demands for racial equality, feminists seeking sexual equality, and doubt in our government's truthfulness and commitment to the common man had never been higher. Sex, drugs, and rock and roll seemed to be the order of the day. But it was also a time of great adventure and excitement for young Americans who were more empowered with rights and privileges than ever before. To be between the ages of eighteen and thirty in the early Seventies was to be part of an age of action. The youth wanted to make a mark in the world, and did not want to wait until they were out of college and had a good paying establishment job like their parents did. They wanted things to happen now. They wanted change. Some demonstrated their rebelliousness with drugs, outrageous dress and anti-establishment writings. Some became even more conservative to counteract their liberal peers. Many dropped out of school and tried to make it on their own in a counter-culture lifestyle of communes and co-ops. Others stayed in school longer, seeking a higher degree so they could be more successful than their already successful parents.

The youth of America were in a time of transition. They knew they were causing changes and they reveled in that knowledge.

I was part of that generation and was at a transitional point in my life. A junior in college, I had just turned twenty-one, and seemed to have my future well planned out. I would graduate, spend four years in the army, and then get a teaching job. But as simple as that seemed to be, there was still much of my life that was in turmoil. Politically, philosophically, socially, and even romantically, I was not sure where I stood or what I really believed. But I can say with certainty that my desires for change, excitement and adventure were centered on getting away, travelling, and seeing more of the world. I wanted to get out there, see it all, and be

Ready to hit the road.

part of it. That was the passion of the Sixties I carried into the early 1970's.

Physically, I was not threatening to anyone when I was twenty-one. I was six feet tall, but thin and lanky, weighing 160 pounds. I had a baby-face and only needed to shave once a week. I kept my hair short and wore rather conservative clothes compared to many in the early Seventies. My young looks seemed to help more than hinder me throughout the summer. Frequently drivers picked me up after passing by other hitchhikers who had long hair, beards, and disheveled cloths. On more than one occasion a driver would say something like "You looked pretty safe to pick up, that's why I stopped."

I have always loved to travel and experience the adventure of seeing new places. But I was never fond of guided tours or professionally booked trips. They were too organized and only showed the best known tourist destinations. The best way to see a place was to experience it as much like the locals as possible; visiting places off the beaten path and seeing how the real people lived. It might not be comfortable or just like home, but that was what I expected when I traveled. I wanted to experience the differences, the culture, and learn the thoughts and ideas of the people and places I visited. That was the fun of traveling to new places.

For me, travel and history went hand in hand. The most interesting part of history depended on where I was, or where I was going. Why did a particular place develop the way it did? Who were the founders of this place? Why did they settle here? What did they do to survive and how did they raise their families? Going out west, I wanted to study the history of the region. Going to Germany, I wanted to know the history of whatever city, palace, cathedral, or city wall I would be looking at. That was the way I learned history. Some was natural curiosity, but much of the desire to travel and learn the history of places came from some strong family influences.

As I sat at my little campsite in the middle of the Iowa cornfield, I thought about my own background and how I had been bitten by that strange bug of wanderlust – the desire to travel and see the world.

My family always had a bit of wanderlust in its blood. We usually blamed my maternal grandmother for the desire to explore and see more places. My grandmother, Mabel Richmond, was twenty-three years old, single, and college educated in 1913 when she decided to go to north central Montana and stake a claim to a homestead. She settled a claim near Chinook, Montana, lived in a small cabin, married Harry Green, and had four children in the vastness of the Great Plains. After thirteen years on the range, tired of fighting droughts and declining cattle prices, Mabel and Harry Green moved back to Michigan - where Harry's parents and siblings lived - and had a fifth child. But within a year Grandpa Green was killed in an accident at a Chicago rail yard, and Mabel was faced with the task of raising the five children herself. She became a teacher, kept the family together through the turmoil of the Great Depression, and watched them grow into successful adults.

Throughout that chaos, the West, the Plains, and the homestead remained a favorite part of my grandmother's life. Whenever we visited Bama, as the grandchildren called Mabel, we would hear stories of the West and the homestead. When asked why she homesteaded, she would say it was for the adventure and desire to be off on her own.

Bama once wrote about her homesteading that, "My grandfather, Rueben Richmond, settled in the Minnesota Territory as soon as land opened up in the 1850s... Someone of each generation of the Richmond family has filed and proved up [settled] on a homestead." She felt she was part of "an enduring passion for the thrills and adventures of pioneering. Surely there were hard times... the burning prairie heat, the bitter storms and cold - but I would gladly welcome them all again to satisfy my enduring passion - homesteading."

A few years ago my family visited the site of the original homestead. It was stark, flat, and barren, but deceptively beautiful in its vast expanse, wide vistas of sunrises and sunsets, with a view of the Rockies on the horizon. We all understood the romantic attachment our grandmother had for the small plot of grassland.

My parents always encouraged that sense of adventure and exploration. Robie, as my mother Rosemond became known, graduated from high school in 1937 at age sixteen. Even with the Great Depression still gripping America, she was able to win a scholarship to attend Western Michigan Normal College (now Western Michigan University). At Western she dated Reed Laughlin, a friend from the neighboring village of Horton. They were married in 1940. My brothers Gary and Fred were born one year apart on February 4, 1942 and 1943 respectively. I came along on February 12, 1950.

My father was a physical education teacher and coach. Mom taught elementary school. When America entered World War II, in December 1941, Dad was teaching and coaching at the small northern Michigan village of Au Gres and Mom was pregnant with Gary. My father was the only male teacher in the small school system so the superintendent asked the draft board to exempt him. "They wanted to maintain a male presence at the school," explained Robie. Over the next six years, my parents moved three times - always to a larger school and a greater coaching opportunity. In 1947 Dad took a teaching and coaching position in Port Huron, Michigan, and that is where they settled down. Dad taught, coached basketball, and eventually became the athletic director at Port Huron High School.

Both parents were products of the Great Depression and World War II. They were rather traditional, careful with their money, cautious, and thoughtful with their decisions. They were conservative, but often much more open-minded than their friends. To them, family was the first priority and they raised my brothers and me to be thoughtful, independent, and self-confident. We were expected to be honest, loyal, and respectful. We were a close-knit family where academics and athletics were equally important. We grew up with the expectation of getting good grades, playing basketball and other sports, and going on to college. Our parents were our role models.

Mom was intellect, idealistic, and a romantic. She was curious and always wanted to know what was around the next corner or over the next rise. Emotional and spontaneous, she was amazed by natural phenomena. She loved sunrises and sunsets and more than once woke me at night to go outside and see the shooting stars or some other celestial event. She was the first feminist I knew - she played ball with us, defended us on the backyard basketball court, and often beat us all in golf. Yet, for all her feminist attitudes, she also taught us to be gentlemen and to respect the "fairer sex". Her boys were expected to hold the door or her chair, take her coat, and to treat her as a lady. We grew up with the understanding that women were special, but also equal, in the family.

Dad was down to earth, logical, and quietly determined. He was patient, rational, and had a proud, adrenaline pumping can-do attitude hidden in his gruff exterior. He rarely lost his temper, but when he did he would explode with anger, then quickly calm down and explain himself. He never had to do much to discipline his sons, as we all feared the look that said he was disappointed in us. From him we learned human equality and to not judge someone by their appearances. The civil rights movement was unnecessary for him, since he did not have any racial prejudices. Dad brought black student-athletes to our house for a meal, or gave them a ride home long before it was socially acceptable. Growing up, we did not think anything of it. That was just the way it was done.

Politically my parents exemplified a simple balance. They rarely talked politics at home, but when they did it was an intellectual discussion, not a passionate one. Mom was more moderate and more progressive in her political thoughts. She had great concern for the underdog. Dad was more conservative. Not necessarily old fashioned, but cautious and slower to accept change. He felt things like racial and sexual equality, educational changes, or international affairs were best solved over time. He believed people wanted changes too fast. He considered himself to be one of President Nixon's "Silent Majority".

But the most important expectation of both parents was that their boys would be independent and self-reliant. They supported our ideas and gave us plenty of opportunities to do things on our own. We were expected to make our own choices and follow through with what we decided. They would support us, and pushed us to make our own way. If we made a mistake, we were expected to learn from it and do better next time. It instilled a sense of confidence and assurance in all of their sons.

My parents always liked to travel, although there were not many chances when they were growing up during the Depression and World War II. There was not much traveling during my early childhood, since Dad and Mom were busy raising three boys on teachers' salaries. When we did travel my mother always made our trips fun and educational –the result of being a third grade teacher. She was a master of word games and explaining the history of city names and locations as we drove back and forth to my grandparents' homes in southern Michigan. During my childhood we made several trips east in the summer. In particular I remember trips to Washington D.C. to visit my aunt and another to Lake Champlain and Montreal to pick up Fred from a basketball camp. On each trip, Mom, with her interest in science, would discuss the geographical formations in the Appalachians and point out the natural beauty of the different areas we drove through. Dad was always interested in stopping at historical spots, battlefields, and fortifications. Throughout all of these adventures I learned to love the history, geography and natural beauty of the eastern United States.

Circumstances developed in 1961 that created more opportunity for the family to travel east. Gary was admitted to the United States Naval Academy in Annapolis, Maryland, as a midshipman. At the same time Fred was admitted to the United States Military Academy in West Point, New York, as a cadet. The family received a considerable amount of notoriety having two sons at the academies. We were not the first family, nor have we been the last, to have sons at the competing academies, however, the unique situation did lead to a number of newspaper reports and interest in their education from the Port Huron public. Over the next four years, my parents and I took a number of trips to Annapolis and West Point. These trips helped me develop a love of history, in particular for the American Civil War. Each trip became an adventure into battlefields, monuments, and personalities. By the time my brothers graduated in June 1965 I was thoroughly engrossed with the history of that era.

Fred, myself, & Gary.
Probably late 1970.

The final catalyst to my wanderlust came in 1965 and 1966 - my sophomore year in high school. That year my parents agreed to host an exchange student from Sweden. Thomas Kierkegaard was a tall, intelligent, athletic, personable Swede who moved in with us and became a beloved member of the family. I did not even mind giving up the solitude of my bedroom, and we learned to share and discuss things as only brothers can. Thomas gave me an international perspective on news and events I had not appreciated before, and he taught me to look at things from both sides of an argument. He gave me a view of life in Sweden and Cold War Europe that could not be found in any American history text or tour book. His opinions on life and events around him helped me mature and see things through different eyes. Thomas loved America, but was passionate about his native land. He was constantly explaining how both countries had things to offer. He was amazed at the wide open land and the woodlands of Michigan, exclaiming how in Sweden they did not have that much land to leave vacant. He was probably the first person I knew who saw the waste Americans produced with their big, gas-guzzling cars, their tendency to leave land untended, and failure to appreciate the beautiful environment around them.

"Look at all that land," he would say. "Why doesn't someone farm it or something?" Or he might comment about a trashy woodland. "In Sweden we would have people clean out that forest."

Thomas's perspective of American politics – coming as it did in the mid Sixties as the U.S. was getting more involved in the Vietnam conflict – made me start to look at our policies and question if our government actually was making the best decisions for the American people.

Thomas's viewpoints caused me to look at things with a more internationalist outlook. This was a very significant time for our family. Fred was in Vietnam as an infantry officer and Gary was an ensign on board a destroyer off the Vietnam coast. Thomas took part in many family discussions about what they were doing and why they were doing it. By the time Thomas returned to Sweden in August of 1966 he was truly another big brother for me to look up to.

That summer my parents decided they wanted to show Thomas the western United States. We took a three week trip out to Yellowstone, Grand Teton, and Rocky Mountain National Parks. This was not only an adventure for Thomas, but also for me, since I had never been west of Chicago and I would be able to drive, having just received my drivers' license. Dad bought a small, used camper trailer with a fold out tent area and a screened in porch. In all, it would create a 10' x 10' sleeping area and another 10' x 10' screened shelter. The trailer was pulled by our big red Pontiac Bonneville station wagon. Thomas and I slept in the tent area and Mom and Dad slept in the back of the wagon, which was big enough for two air mattresses.

We headed west on Interstate 90, taking in all the tourist spots of South Dakota – the Corn Palace in Mitchell, Wall Drugs, The Badlands, and of course Mount Rushmore – before heading on to Yellowstone. It was not only the history and uniqueness of these stops that infatuated me, but the stark beauty of the landscape, the harsh environment, and the differences apparent in the way people lived their lives. I have fond memories of sitting around the campfire and watching the stars. Mom would point out the constellations, while Dad would remark on the western culture and scenery with a couple of astute comments. Thomas asked questions about American history and lifestyles, and we all quietly enjoyed the situation.

Thomas was fascinated by the West and the wide open spaces, and his appreciation of the place only increased my own feelings. He loved hiking, climbing, and exploring the smallest spot. Once, in Yellowstone, when an unwary woman screamed in panic that she had seen this tall young man "just go over the side of the cliff" and probably fall to his death, Dad – knowing exactly who it was – just calmly walked over to the edge and yelled, "Thomas get up here before you scare someone else and get us in trouble with the rangers!"

As the trip continued on into Grand Teton National Park, then down through Wyoming to Rocky Mountain National Park, Mom told us about life on the Montana plains and Bama's stories about the homestead. Although my mother was only five when they left the range, it made an impact on her for the rest of her life. In Colorado we met up with the rest of the "Chinook Coyotes," as Mom's relatives liked to call themselves. My uncles, Charlie and Bob, in particular, filled me with stories about the homestead, and even had a brand made up – the Z/T brand that Harry Green had used on his cattle.

When we returned home I was filled with images of the West and wanted to know more. Any historical book on the western movement, the Oregon Trail, the gold rushes, fur trappers, Native Americans, or anything else about the West became fodder for reading and studying. The history of the West became a passion from that point on. And the stories of my grandmother's homesteading became much more personal and relevant.

After high school graduation in 1968, I wanted to travel more and see new places. Any chance to travel that came along, I took advantage of it. The opportunity to see new places, meet people, learn about different cultures, and discover the history of places fascinated me. By the time I started at the University of Michigan in the fall, I already had a list of places I wanted to see, beginning with another trip to the West and a visit to Sweden to see Thomas's world. The wanderlust started by my grandmother Mabel, and expanded by my mother, was the seed for my summer adventure and brought me to that Iowa cornfield.

The Rules of the Road

"He was alone. He was unheeded, happy, and near to the wild heart of life. He was alone and young and willful and wild-hearted..."
James Joyce - From <u>On The Loose</u>, by Terry and Renny Russell

In 1968, during my freshman year at Michigan, my friend, Randy Sharp, introduced me to a small book, <u>On the Loose</u>, published by the Sierra Club and written by two young men, Renny and Terry Russell, about their travels through the American West. The book was a collection of their reflections on the beauty of nature and the magnificence of what they saw on their hikes. It emphasized man's relationship with the environment, how we had affected it, and how we could learn to live within that environment. It was a very simple book, with photographs taken by the brothers, but it had a deeper, more romantic message of love and appreciation of nature. There was an undeniable bond between the boys and the world around them. This uncluttered, straightforward book became a philosophical bible for me. The simple message seemed clear to me and it was the only reading material I took on the journey. The quote above seemed appropriate as I started the first leg - thus, it made its way into the journal. I love the words, rhythm and rhyme of that little book. I still have it and reread it.

By the late 1960s hitchhiking had become a socially acceptable way of traveling with its own rules and system of etiquette. There were thousands of American youth hitchhiking. Each summer young people - mostly males, but also some females - would travel throughout the United States, Canada, and most of Western Europe by hitchhiking. It was cheap, exciting and relatively safe. Far fewer young people owned cars and the United States did not have dependable public transportation. For many, thumbing through Europe was a rite of passage. Today, I still meet many of my generation who fondly remember experiences hitchhiking during their college years.

Of course hitchhiking has been around ever since the automobile came along, with the famous scene in the movie *It Happened One Night* with Clark Gable and Claudette Colbert trying to hitch a ride. Dad told me many stories of hitching rides from Kalamazoo and Western Michigan College to his hometown of Horton in the 1930's and both Gary and Fred had done some hitchhiking before me. Most of my experiences had been from Ann Arbor to Port Huron, and those trips taught me many tricks of the trade before I ventured further. There were many times where patience and a little prayer got me through some sticky situations, but I never felt seriously threatened or in danger.

While there are not as many hitchhikers today as there were forty years ago, the rules of the road are still the same. To be a successful hitchhiker required being a bit of a gambler, being a quick study of personalities, and having a willingness to live on the edge. When a driver stopped to pick you up, it required a quick decision about the safety and an understanding of where they are going. Were they going to help you along your way? Did they look helpful and honest? Did the car look safe? Did the driver look safe? All those questions and more had to be digested and analyzed within a few seconds before you got in the car. I learned quickly and felt confident in my ability to see the answers to those questions.

Anyone who has done much hitchhiking has a story or two about getting picked up by drunks, being taken off your route as a practical joke, waiting hours for a ride, or being dropped off in an undesirable location. You always made a mental escape plan to get out quickly if things were not going well. I had my share of rides sitting amongst empty beer cans, or heading down strange roads. I always thought about how to get out at the first stop sign or street light if needed. There were plenty of days when I stood so long at one spot I thought of giving up, but someone always came along just in time.

The most interesting situation I remember occurred during the spring of my freshman year at the University of Michigan. I was trying to hitchhike home from Ann Arbor to Port Huron, which was about a hundred miles.

I did not leave until almost sundown on a Friday night. Everything went fine at first. I was picked up outside of Ann Arbor by a fellow who was going to Detroit. What I did not understand was that he was going right downtown, and soon I found myself dropped off on Gratiot Avenue in the middle of the Detroit ghetto. It was about ten o'clock, very dark, and I appeared to be the only white boy around. I became nervous about when and where my next ride was going to come from. Only two years earlier, in 1967, this part of Detroit had exploded into some of the deadliest race riots in American history. It definitely was on my mind that night! Suddenly a large Cadillac pulled up with two large African American men inside. They rolled down the window, looked at me and said, "A white boy like you can't be down here at this time of night! Where you think your goin'?"

I very meekly said, "I'm - huh- trying to get to Port Huron," while trying to assess the situation and my possible options.

"Well get your ass in here. We'll take you there."

"All the way? That would be great!"

With that I climbed in the back seat. These two gentlemen laughed and talked about me as if I wasn't even there, but took me fifty miles out of their way and dropped me off about two blocks from home. I learned a valuable lesson to never judge people based on the place or situation.

By my junior year in college I had done a lot of hitchhiking. I felt so confident in my ability to get rides I would just take off when the weather was nice. One Memorial Day weekend I awoke on Saturday to a lovely spring day and predictions of good weather. I decided to hitchhike south just to see how far I could get in a day. By Saturday evening – and about four rides later – I was just outside Lexington, Kentucky, and decided to stop for the night. I slipped through a fence, found a nice quiet spot in a distant corner under a group of trees, and lay down. The next morning I awoke to find myself in the middle of a Kentucky horse farm and surrounded by a group of beautiful thoroughbred horses grazing in the field. While appreciating the beauty and serenity of the surroundings, I realized I did not want to get caught trespassing, climbed over the fence and headed back north on I-75. By the end of the day I was back in Ann Arbor telling stories of my little adventure.

Hitchhiking required a great amount of patience, optimism, and faith in your fellow man. When picked up, you always wanted to greet your driver with a smile and an optimistic, cooperative attitude. Wherever they were going and however far they could take you was fine - you did not have much luck when you tried to impose your desires on them.

There were some basic unwritten rules to life on the road. First of all, you did not take another hiker's place in line. If you arrived at an expressway ramp or the major crossroads of a two lane road, you allowed any hitchhikers who are there first to stay at the front and you patiently went to the end of the line. If you got picked up and there were others in line, you might mention to the driver to pick up another rider.

Hitchhiking also demanded more walking than most would believe. While you might wait for a ride on a highway entrance ramp, getting there usually meant you had to do some walking. You were frequently dropped off somewhere else and had to walk to the ramp. Even more walking was necessary if you were on a two-lane road. The first order of business was to find a good spot for people to stop, and that might entail a lengthy stroll before you got to the perfect spot. The other reason to keep walking was that some places considered it vagrancy or loitering if you stayed at one spot too long. So you walked slowly and patiently so as not to be considered a vagrant. You would do anything possible to avoid unnecessary contact with the local authorities.

Occasionally the police would stop and ask for identification and a destination. Although hitchhiking was illegal in most states there were so many hitchhikers on the interstate it was impractical to ticket or arrest them. The police were lenient as long as hitchers were not on the highway and did not create traffic problems. There were lots of stories among the hitchhikers of tough police and hikers being harassed, arrested, or just chased off the roadway. It became obvious the longer I was on the road that there was a prejudice among many police organizations against "long-haired hippie freaks". I maintained a short haircut and was clean shaven, but it was not unusual to see the police harass long haired hitchhikers, then pass right by me, even though I may have been only a hundred yards from the other hiker. It also is significant, looking back, that I saw very few African-American or Hispanic hitchhikers in those days. The prejudice against them by police and society in general must have made their chances of getting a ride very slim.

When the cops did stop me they would ask for identification and then radio into the office for a background check. There was the possibility of being taken to the station for something. That would have cost time and money, so I wanted to avoid that. Since I did not have a police record, it was comforting to hear the "No record" come over the radio.

When hitchhiking, you wanted to have as little baggage as possible so the person picking you up would not be inconvenienced loading up a bunch of bags. As the trip went on, I purged unnecessary things from my bags, trying to make them as light and unobtrusive as possible. Many hitchers would carry a sign stating a specific destination, which could sometimes be beneficial and sometimes not. Signs could tell the driver your specific destination, but in my case, where I was just "going west" to no particular destination each day, a sign was unnecessary and could be confusing to the driver.

When picked up it was normal for you to initiate some small talk to break the ice with the driver and any other passengers. I quickly fell into what would become the normal routine while on the road. My first couple rides out of Ann Arbor were rather short - 20 to 40 miles - and the conversation usually went something like this:

"Where ya headed?"

"Goin west," I'd say. "I'll go as far as you are going down the highway. I'm on my way to San Francisco. I've got an aunt there I'm going to visit."

"Well, okay - Climb in, I'll take you down the road a bit."

"Great, every little bit will help."

"You doing this all by yourself?"

"Yeah - I like to travel solo. Then I can make my own schedule and stops."

The conversation then moved to how I expected to take five or six days getting out west, how I planned to stay in campgrounds along the way, how I was a student at the University of Michigan, and other trivial things. I usually did not bring up ROTC Summer Camp right away in the discussion. The topic of ROTC could bring out some strong political ideology either for or against the military and the Vietnam War, so I did not mention it until I had some indication of how the driver felt about those topics.

Some drivers were very conversational and wanted to talk about any topic that came up - it was their way of passing time as they drove - and others were content to get the basic bits of information then drive on in silence. Then there the drivers who just seemed absolutely engrossed in what you were doing and why you were hitchhiking at all. Early, on my first day on the road, I was picked up by two young teenage girls who were astonished anyone would want to hitchhike to the west coast.

"You mean you're going to go all the way to California by hitchhiking?" They exclaimed between adolescent giggles. "Aren't you going to get lonely? Aren't you going to get hungry? Where will you sleep? Aren't you afraid?"

The questions seemed to be fired out in one fast steady stream and never gave me a chance to respond. When they paused to catch their breath and giggled a little more I answered each of their questions as best I could with my rather rehearsed answers. It seemed to cure their curiosity a little bit, but not entirely.

"You're like a professional hitchhiker, aren't you?" One of them breathlessly exclaimed.

"Well, I guess in a way I am." I relented. They giggled and laughed at the thought of hitchhiking for a living. I let them have their fun, since they were taking me down the road another forty miles. I figured their expression of being a "professional hitchhiker" seemed appropriate for the moment.

When your next ride, and the day's successful travel, depended on how you interacted with different people, different places, and different situations, you learned to be quiet, agreeable, and observant of people's questions and body language. Through it all - with a variety of drivers who were personable, spontaneous, optimistic, pessimistic, quiet, or even grouchy - hitchhiking taught me a great deal about people and the world around me.

After my first night on the road and a surprisingly good sleep in the cornfield, I awoke to a brilliant Great Plains sunrise. My makeshift campsite had been perfect and I felt well rested. It was still early and a light fog filtered the sunbeams and reflected the dew on the corn stalks around me. I pondered the beauty of the field for a few minutes then realized I had better be going before the farm owner started making his rounds. I walked back to the highway, stuck out my thumb, and started my second day on the road.

Again the most memorable ride of day two was in a big rig with a driver named Kenny. He took me from Des Moines, Iowa to Lincoln, Nebraska and along the way I learned much more about the long haul trucking business. I discovered being a cross country trucker was a lot of hard work punctuated by hours of rather boring driving. The truck cabs were hot, stuffy, and the ride was often very uncomfortable. The drivers were frequently crude, opinionated and a bit perverted.

"Hey, check this one out," Kenny stated as things got boring along Interstate 80. With that he slowed enough to allow a car with a good looking young lady pass the truck. The cab was up so high that when she passed he could look down and see her legs.

"Whoa, she's a hot one. Take a look for yourself," and he proceeded to speed up and pass the young lady. And yep - I did have a good look at a nice set of legs.

"My turn!" he exclaimed as he slowed down again and allowed her to pass on his side. This continued back and forth until he had passed her about three times. She eventually became annoyed and sped away. I suppose it was sexist and perverted, but at the time I felt it was just a way for the driver to get a little variety in his boring day and get a cheap thrill as he was barreling down the interstate.

Kenny stopped at a truck stop for lunch and offered to buy me a hamburger, which I quickly accepted. He was a bit crude, but friendly and entertaining, so I enjoyed being with him. After lunch, however, we discovered his cab had been broken into. There wasn't much missing, just a few of Kenny's favorite music tapes (No CDs in those days) and my sunglasses. We cursed the thief and continued down the road, but I missed those sunglasses and squinted into the sun for the rest of the trip. I did not replace them until I reached San Francisco.

Typically the truck drivers and I had lots of discussions about college life, where I was going, what I was doing, and what my plans were. They were surprisingly diverse in their political opinions. My stereotype of the typical truck driver was of a politically conservative individual, but many of them expressed opposition to the war. Some, like Joe, were Vietnam veterans who had taken up truck driving when they got home. They seemed to appreciate my wanderlust because their job required a love of traveling too. Overall, I found the truckers to be observant and honest. They viewed life from the top of their cab and did not miss much that went on around them.

I took a quick side trip off the interstate into Lincoln, Nebraska to see what was there, and then got right back on the road. That turned out to be an uninteresting two hour diversion. I'm not sure why I wanted to see Lincoln. Maybe I thought it would be exciting because it was a college town. Or maybe I thought there might be some cool historical site to visit - neither was true. Most of all, it was just an example of my laid back "I'll go where you are going" attitude on that second day, since it was where my driver was headed. Afterwards I realized how my attitude was not always the best and it could keep me from getting where I wanted to go.

My final rides got me to Pioneer Village outside Minden, Nebraska. With a kitschy pioneer museum and a cheap campground, it was a good stop for the night. Day two ended after almost 350 miles. I was happy with my progress.

May 28:

Only about 350 miles today, some good rides though. Iowa was nice, but Nebraska is something else! The flatness from Lincoln on is awe inspiring. Lincoln is a nice city, strikingly rises out of the prairies. U. of Nebraska looks like a nice school. Another beautiful day for hitching. Damn though, lost my sunglasses (stolen a better word for it!) [At a] truck stop, Kenny put them on the dash. When we got back they, and a few other little things, were gone. I'm going to miss those badly.

I'm on the Oregon Trail now. Sure would like to have seen it 150 years ago. The farms here are just amazing, so big and so flat. Interesting land. Endlessly flat. Missed Kearney Historical Park, but got a good place to shower and get comfortable for the road. The road goes on, gotta stick to it. (1st police check today)

DRIVERS - DAY 2

13. Homestead – Des Moines = "Conservation Freak" – going to Iowa City & Dallas. Kittens, funny

14. To Omaha – Kenny – Trucker. Lost my shades, damn!

15. Through Omaha

16. To Lincoln – businessman

17 & 18. Into Lincoln & Out. Nice town

19. Lincoln to Kearney = Opel Kadet. Classy

20. To Minden & Pioneer Village = Teacher from Santa Barbara on leave

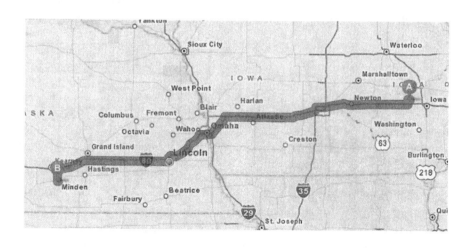

A Time of Transition

Looking back, it is significant I made the trip in 1971. I'm not sure I would have been able to make the journey and experience the culture and society of America as easily or candidly at any other time in our history. In my lifetime the circumstances have never been quite the same. I realize now that our nation – and the whole world for that matter – was in a period of great transition. The post-World War II world was changing. Most of our social mores were changing. The stable, prosperous, and family oriented world of the 1950's was giving way to the more independent, less stable world of the 1970's and 1980s. No longer was the *Father Knows Best* or *Leave it to Beaver* image of America the social norm. The protests and changes of the Civil Rights Movement and the anti-war movement had destroyed much of the image of American prosperity and stability of the 1950's. The men and women who had lived through the Depression and won WWII were still in positions of power politically and economically, but socially and culturally a new generation was beginning to have an impact. The post WWII generation – the Baby Boomers – had grown up with more money, more education, and more job security than their parents, and they were not going to wait before they were heard and made their impact on the direction of the United States.

We were restless, curious, and unsatisfied with the way things were. The old answer of "It's always been this way..." did not satisfy us. We were seeking something different. We were not sure what or where we would find it, but we knew we wanted more than our parent's generation had. We wanted to see the world and learn from what we saw. It was a great time to be young because there were many opportunities available to us. It may not have seemed like it then, but looking back it is clear to see the Baby Boomer generation had more advantages and opportunities than any generation before or since.

Politically, the Baby Boomers were still too young to affect politics by being elected to office. But they did make themselves heard. They created one of the most democratic times in our history as they insisted on voicing their opinions and demands. Sometimes this resulted in destructive protests and violence, such as the rioting and violence that occurred at the Democratic National Convention in Chicago in 1968, where anti-establishment protesters were violently confronted by hundreds of police and National Guard troops. But many more subtle changes also took place. For example, the passage of the 26th Amendment giving eighteen year olds the right to vote came about because that segment of society was becoming so involved in the political landscape. Politicians wanted them involved in their party politics. Today, gaining the youth vote is vital to any politician's success.

Perhaps the biggest political change of this period was a lack of trust in politicians and the political system. By the early Seventies the issue of Vietnam, civil rights, the economy and many other problems that seemed unsolvable by the politicians, had made young Americans impatient and distrustful of the government. And this was before Watergate. This impatience with the political system transcended the political parties of the young and affected everyone.

The Baby Boomers made their biggest impact on the changing times in culture and society. The growth, and slow acceptance, of the Youth Culture of rock and roll, drugs, independence, and "searching for something new" was starting to become an accepted part of America. Many youth in America no longer wanted to just follow their family traditions. They did not want the routine of marriage, job, and family their parents had presented to them. At least not right away. While that may have been their ultimate goal, they still wanted to look around and experience life before they settled down, married, and had a family. I know that was my plan. I wanted to experience society and culture. I wanted to have the independence to travel and learn before I went into the army and became more established in life.

There are many books and studies about the Hippies and the Love Generation and how they changed the American landscape. By the early Seventies, that part of society had become much more accepted. While many of the more conservative elements of society felt the youth culture was wrong and a disgrace to our nation, they still begrudgingly realized it was here to stay. Consequently, wherever I went in 1971, a segment of society accepted my wanderlust and was willing to support it and help me out on the way.

Things were also different then as far as safety and crime were concerned. It was a time of more innocence and community feeling than today. There were very few instances of travelers being harmed or violated. Occasionally I would talk to a hitchhiker who had been driven out of their way, or dropped off somewhere inconvenient, but those were seen as practical jokes or tricks on the traveler – not as malicious crimes. Hitchhiking was an accepted way to travel – even promoted and described in "How To" books and pamphlets. Wherever I went there were hikers on the road. My drivers might be old or young, conservative or liberal, male or female (although predominantly male) but they still regarded me as a safe passenger with whom they could converse and exchange ideas. Things seemed to be friendly, open, and innocent.

The Oregon Trail, Cowboys & Friends

"Now I see the secret of making the best persons,
It is to grow in the open air and eat and
sleep with the earth."
- Walt Whitman
From <u>On The Loose</u> by Terry and Renny Russell

My second night was spent at Pioneer Village, a tourist campground and museum near Minden, Nebraska. It was a nice, comfortable place to spend the night, and the next morning I had a pleasant surprise while talking to the owner. He decided that since I had not taken up a full campsite, he would not charge me the full camping rate. He was just another in a long string of people who wanted to help their fellow man in small ways.

One of my first rides was with a young man who was driving straight through to Denver from Minnesota. He had been driving all night and asked me to drive so he could sleep. It was not unusual for someone to pick me up so they could sleep, or have someone to talk to so they would not doze off. The fact that this driver saw me as an opportunity to sleep and not as any type of threat, said a lot about the innocence and trust people had at the time. I was pleased to drive, but he thought it was strange I did not want to go all the way to Denver with him. I had decided I was going to take my time and see things I was interested in, and the Oregon Trail was tops on my list. Because of some nice long rides, I was a bit further west than planned, so I had time to explore and do some thinking.

This was one of the most interesting days of the summer. I got off Interstate 80 and headed northwest on US 26 toward Scotts Bluff, Nebraska and Guernsey, Wyoming. I was in the high plains. I was on the Oregon Trail - the subject of many of my favorite books and fantasies. The vastness of the prairie and the wild nature of the land were apparent, even within the confines of modern settlements. The sky stretched from horizon to horizon without interruption or obstruction from trees and buildings. This was the land of the Sioux, the buffalo, the Mountain Men, and the homesteaders. This was the Great Plains my grandmother had fallen in love with back in 1913 and the land my mother was born into. And although the wild grasslands were replaced by endless fields of corn and wheat, it was still easy to sense how this land must have impressed and engulfed the early settlers.

In his famous "Frontier Thesis" developed in 1893, historian Frederick Jackson Turner laid the basis of

America's idealized vision of the American west. "The existence of an area of free land, its continuous recession, and the advance of American settlement westward explain American development...The frontier," he claimed, "is the line of most rapid Americanization." The need to develop the frontier led to American innovation, greater freedom, increased democracy, and a special sort of "rugged individualism". Historians still debate Turner's thesis, but his ideas fit into my vision of the West in 1971. It was a land of history and mystery. It was a land of ever changing beauty, from the vastness of the plains, to the threatening openness of the desert, and to the majesty of the mountains. It was a place where the people could be themselves without the constraints of society and still be accepted for who they were and what they did. The West was where a man or woman could go, start over, and become a success in life. This was exciting, and being there was an important part of my growth and maturation.

I had read and studied much about the West and western expansion. While other college kids read mysteries or science fiction for relaxation, I read about the Mountain Men like Jedediah Smith and Kit Carson. The stories of the Oregon Trail and the people who forged their way west were thrilling to me. The California Gold Rush, the building of the Transcontinental Railroad, the Pony Express and homesteading were all topics that grabbed my attention. To me, the West was a place of individual effort, strength and determination. It represented the individuality and freedom I was seeking on my own excursion. It seemed to be the most exciting era in American history. Ideals and self-determination could work hand-in-hand to make a better society and culture out of a barren and harsh land. In my opinion, Western art was the greatest example of American artistry and reflected the inner beauty of the great American landscape.

My impressions of the West were romanticized and unrealistic. I glossed over the hardships and failures that were a significant part of the West's history. The deaths from fatigue and exposure on the trails, the lawlessness in the early towns, or the examples of racism toward Asians did not upset me. Even the fact that my own grandparents had to leave their Montana homestead due to crop failures and declining cattle prices did not deter my romantic image of the American West. The terrible treatment of the Native Americans by the white settlers, or the prejudice and aggressive-ness toward Mexicans the ideas of Manifest Destiny created, all seemed to be part of the story of the West. And I did not really understand or appreciate the environmental damage done by mining and hunting of the early settlers. To me, that was part of the great symphony of the American settlement of the frontier.

So when I came to a spot like Scotts Bluff, Register Cliff, and ruts from the Oregon Trail, I felt a personal connection to the history I had read. I was following the route of the western emigrants and it seemed to come to life as I saw the land. I loved seeing the trails and the views of the West and wondering what life must have been like for early pioneers. I looked at a stream in the mountains and wondered if it had changed since the first mountain men had come to trap. When I saw abandoned mine sites, I did not see the manmade damage to the earth; I saw the lives of the miners, the new riches for our nation, and the development of society. The West symbolized everything good about America - beautiful vistas, wide open spaces, freedom, independence, individual growth, and opportunity.

Even today the West seems to have its own mystique. The unique beauty of the plains, the mountains, the deserts, and the big skylines create a feeling of being one with nature. And the people who live in the West love to maintain the attitude of independence and self-reliance. They tend to be more rebellious and more willing to fight to maintain their freedoms and privacy. There is a greater sense of belonging to the land and nature. The distances and desolation of some places in the western states are greater than in the eastern U.S. and it creates a different type of citizen. Although today's United States is more united than ever before by television, the internet, and politics, the West still prides itself in being a little different, a little more sassy, and much more independent. The ideas of Jackson's "frontier thesis" of "freedom", "innovation" and "rugged individualism" still hold true as much as they did at the turn of the century.

Hitchhiking and traveling on my own created many opportunities for self-examination and time to notice the minute things I may have missed in a more hurried situation.   I studied farm landscapes.   I looked at fencing.   I watched the birds.   I even calculated how many telephone poles there were in a mile.   In my journal I mentioned a horse I observed while waiting on the roadside.   I had seen many horses before, but the fact I wrote about this horse is indicative of how much more aware of the surroundings I was becoming.   Or maybe it indicates I stood at one spot on the roadside for too long and was getting a little stir-crazy.   The simplicity of the journal statement probably says more about my awakening than it does about the beauty of the horse.

The horse of Oshkosh, Neb.

There were some very interesting rides at this point. Now I was off the interstate highway the rides came from a different type of person than before.   I was off the route most hitchhikers took west and most of the day I was the only thumber on the road. There were more short rides of five to ten miles and a very eclectic group of drivers. All my rides that afternoon were with people who were just going to, or from, work, or doing their daily errands. They were enjoyable because they were local and had different attitudes from the long distance drivers of the first few days. There were farmers who explained life on a Nebraska ranch, and youth who had never been anywhere except their immediate surroundings. The one comment consistently made was how important water was in that part of the country. Coming from Michigan with plenty of rain and where water was not a problem, it was a topic I had never thought about.

The most symbolic ride of farming country was the ride in the back of a flatbed truck filled with chickens in cages and a pile of manure. I had been standing on the roadside for about thirty minutes when a truck pulled over.

"I'll give you a ride if you don't mind sitting in back," the driver said. The cab was already full of farm workers.

"Yeah, that's fine with me," I said without thinking about it. Only after I climbed in the back of the truck did I notice the chickens. I found a small spot to sit and climbed in. Then, as the truck started moving, I noticed the manure. It was not a huge pile, but it was a smelly mess and the wind blowing through the back of the truck made the smell worse. Luckily the ride was only for about five miles before they turned off to go to their farm, so I was not there for too long. But for the rest of the day I was very conscious of smelling like chicken shit! When I got to Scotts Bluff National Monument I spent about ten minutes in the rest room trying to wash off the smell. I felt dirty the rest of the day.

From Scotts Bluff to Guernsey, Wyoming, I had another group of interesting drivers, and none of them seemed to notice the manure smell, so I worried about it less. One driver was a hermit-type preacher who seemed to reinforce the fact I was out west where a full beard, a quiet disposition, and a huge respect for an individual's privacy seemed to be the theme of the day. I met a Japanese tourist helping his friend walk the Oregon Trail who was even more obsessed with the western movement than I was. Then there was the thirty-something man who I convinced to go to Fort Laramie, Wyoming. I wanted to see the fort, since it was a key spot on the western movement, but already knew it did not have any place to stay and would be closed by the time we got there. Even so, I told him there was a campground nearby. He took me about ten miles out of his way only to discover everything was closed. I apologized and he took me into Guernsey, where there was a state park. I felt a little selfish and guilty about having him drive by Fort Laramie, but I also wanted to see the famous outpost of the frontier and it seemed to be the only chance I would have to do that.

May 29:

Nice way to wake up – walking to the john I met Harold Warp, owner of Pioneer Village. He decided that since I took up such little area – to give me back $1.00 of the $1.50 camping fee! Went past Fort Kearney.

[I] drove across Neb. for a guy while he tried to sleep. Missed the rain, guess I was lucky. Got off at Ogallala. Could have gone with him into Denver, but I passed him, and another to Denver, in favor of U.S.26 (about 300 miles out of my way) and the Oregon Trail. Why? Can't really say, but then why did I hitch-hike at all?

The land was cool – got into my first bluffs and buttes. I really felt like a pioneer and like walking. Oshkosh, and a beautiful horse! Wow! Damn trucker took me off the Trail and I couldn't quite go by Chimney Rock – but I saw it and the rest of the landmarks [in the distance]. They are truly fantastic formations. Went to Scott's [sic] Bluff Natl. Monument. It completely engulfed me in history. I could just feel the urge of the pioneer and see the wagons. Those people had something no people or generation has ever come close to matching. To cross this entire continent completely on foot without anywhere to turn – forward and onward. Once they got started they couldn't stop. It wasn't just stamina or enthusiasm – but some hidden, unknown, source of strength kept them together, and always pushing onward towards a singular goal. Maybe it was the goal that was the secret. To have one UNIFIED goal that they could reinforce each other with. Could that be it? Could that be what we're missing? Whatever it was, it was great! I'd like to have some of it.

The Bluffs were most interesting and impressive. But I was impressed and envious of my ride back to the highway. [With me] was a Japanese who was WALKING the Oregon Trail. (Maybe he had some of whatever it is — but he also had help around whenever he wanted or

The Oregon Trail at Scotts Bluff. On the back of this photo I wrote,

"The road west - the physical tracks left by the farmer travelers. The mental and psychological tracks run much deeper. The work, the effort, the constant strain and danger. The bravery and the adventurous frontier spirit that spread through America and was climaxed and brought together on this trail. The road west - how many passed over it - how many didn't - and how many died trying??"

needed it.) It had taken him 27 days to go from Kansas City to Scott's Bluff. He figured about 20 – 24 mi. a day. Boy was I envious in a way.

Guernsey was a small western town, but it had been a stopping spot on the trails west and it had a large state park which sounded inviting. I stepped into a phone booth and made my collect call home.

"Collect call for Tom Laughlin from Guernsey, Wyoming," the operator said to my father.

"Sorry, he isn't here," my father said so they wouldn't be charged for the call. Now they knew where I was and that I was safe.

I started walking to the state park. I had not gone far when a car with three teenage boys offered me a ride. Of course, I accepted.

The driver, Art Kennedy, was a small, lithe sixteen year old with average looks but a wonderful instinct about people. He did not appear to be a cowboy or a tough guy - he was just a personable kid riding around with his buddies looking for something to do. In the end, he not only gave me a ride but also unexpected hospitality. It became an evening of simple honesty, trustworthiness and wholesome friendship.

When I climbed in the backseat of the 1963 Ford and explained my situation, the boys offered to show me around some of the local sights. They nonchalantly offered me a beer from their cooler and explained what life was like as a teenager in Guernsey. It sounded very familiar to many other teenage laments about their hometown. "Boring," "nothin' to do," "same old shit every day," seemed like it could have been said by any teenager anywhere, any time. Yet these young men seemed to have a special appreciation of the land around them and wanted to be out in the wild instead of going to some big city for adventure. They wanted to be part of nature.

When my fascination with the Oregon Trial came up in conversation, they took me to see Register Cliffs, a spot outside of town where you could still see wagon ruts and where pioneers had scratched their names into the rock formations. The pioneer emigrants had signed the cliff to have a record of their journey west and well over one hundred years later their names and dates of passage were still clearly visible. It was a remarkable record of their hard work and determination to get west. I enjoyed seeing the signatures and appreciated how Art and his friends went out of their way to entertain me. They were easygoing, relaxed and happy to show me around their hometown.

As twilight approached, Art headed to the state park so I could get situated for the evening. Just as we got to the park entrance a huge thunderstorm arose. High winds and violent lightning strikes made the prospect of camping very worrisome.

"Hey, you can't camp in this crap," Art said. "Come on over to my house. You can spend the night with us." He had only known me for about an hour, yet he was confident enough to trust me to spend the night.

This faith was inherited from his parents, who proved to be just as friendly and hospitable as their son. When Art brought me in and introduced me, his mother quickly said, "Well of course you're staying for dinner. Think nothing of it," as she set another place at the table.

"We've got that extra bed upstairs," added Art's father. "You're welcome to stay. Art can take you to the highway in the morning when he goes out to the range."

"But Dad that means he's got to get up with me at 4:00 a.m.," exclaimed Art.

"Well, I'm an early riser," I said, "What's up? Why do you have to get up so early?"
"I work on a friend's ranch," Art said. "It's about an hour and a half drive and I have to be there at 6:00, so I have to get up early."

"You mean like a regular cowboy?" I innocently asked.

"Yeah - I ride the range and help keep track of the cattle. This whole area is open range territory so the cattle can be scattered all over. I have to track them down then drive them back to the main herd. I'll be in the back country of Wyoming for about a week driving the cattle. It's hard work, but it's great being out in the open country and it's good pay."

By this time I had developed a considerable amount of trust and rapport with the entire family. Getting up early with Art was never a question.

It's significant, looking back, that Art Kennedy was one of the few drivers whose name I recorded in my journal, and he is the only person with his full name. This young man came to symbolize the innocence and faith of youth. Art never doubted my intentions, never worried I might rob him or his family. In 1971 a person could just be himself and not be questioned about sexual orientation, criminal background, or personal preferences. The Kennedys took me in and offered peaceful shelter from the storm. Without question or controversy they accepted me for who I was and nothing more. They were glad to help out another person. To me, they will always be an example of the Golden Rule in action. Art's simple purity and innocence will always be in my memory.

May 29 continued:

Made it from Fort Kearney to Fort Laramie (and beyond) in one day. Wonder how many it took "them"? Kinda tricked my driver into going by the fort. [It was] closed! It looked disappointing. But got a ride to Guernsey. Picked up by Art Kennedy and friends. What can I say about that kid! Entertained me, gave me a beer, took me to the Trail sights, and gave me a roof over my head out of the rain. He (and his family) were super great people.

Extremely interesting day. Another police check. Feels good to have "No Record" come over the radio. Did quite a bit of walking today. Funny, first day out I could only walk about 2 blocks without resting because of my pack. Today it hardly bothered me at all. The human body is amazing. Great day – guess I'm doing OK.

DRIVERS - DAY 3

21. Back to I-80 = Farmer

22. Guy going to Denver from Minn. I drove, he slept. Got off at Ogallala

23. Kids through Ogallala

24. To Oshkosh, Neb. w/farmer

25. Trucker to Scott's Bluff – quiet guy

26. Into Scott's Bluff in the back of a farm truck sitting in manure!

27. To Bluff Natl Mon = no brakes

28. From Mon to US 26 – little Jap – Keith – had a friend from Tokyo WALKING the Oregon Trail!

29 – 31. Short rides with kids & a farmer

32. Henry, Neb to Torrington, WY. = Guy looked like a complete hermit or something – dirty, bearded, dark tan, etc. He was a preacher!

33. Torrington to Guernsey = Guy & wife & 2 little girls. Kinda tricked him into taking me to Ft Laramie then to Guernsey.

34. Art Kennedy = Great kid – drove all over, telling about his cars, women, etc. 16 yrs old. Poor family kinda made good – interesting. Rode the range – let me stay w/ him that night (rain) – next morning (4:00) to me to Wheatland (wish I'd gone farther)

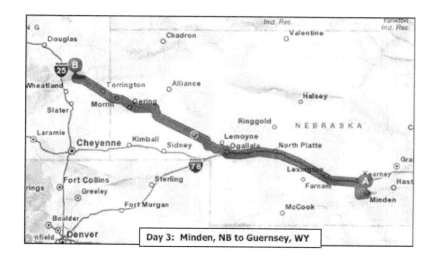

Day 3: Minden, NB to Guernsey, WY

Finding Religion

The experiences of May 30, 1971 impacted me in many ways. If it is possible to establish one day in which my belief in God was established, then that was the day. I awoke early with Art and my adrenaline was already running. I sensed it was going to be an unusual day. A large part of the excitement was the idea of learning more about Art's life as a cowboy and seeing a small part of a lifestyle which I had always heard about, but was foreign to me.

We had a quick breakfast and headed out. Within a short time Art came to his turn-off and I had a decision to make. I could stay with him and go cross country on a little used country road, or stay on the highway. Fearing I may be stranded in the back country, I chose to stay on Interstate 25. We had not had much time to talk, but Art's excitement about his role as a wrangler was contagious and made me envy his freedom.

I soon had another ride with a cowboy who heightened my fascination with the land. Like Art, he seemed to have a personal attachment to the rugged landscape and openness of eastern Wyoming. He was heading down the interstate, and was going to work the open range north of Cheyenne. After the standard introductory questions and answers, he commented on his love of the land.

"I grew up here. The land is just part of my life. When I'm out on the range I'm at peace with the world - I don't have to worry about politics, war, businesses, love, hate, or any of that stuff. I'm free, I'm surrounded by some of the most beautiful scenery in the world, and I just have to take care of myself."

"Aren't there other cowboys out there with you? Don't you guys have a time schedule and responsibilities?" I asked.

"Oh, yeah. But we understand and know each other very well. We all love the freedom and independence of being out on the range - and we don't mess with that. We work as a team, and of course we have to keep an eye on the cattle. We have to stay focused and we are responsible for the herd and what they are doing." He paused and looked out the window to the open range land that ran along the interstate. "It's long hours, hard physical work, and you're at the mercy of Mother Nature - it's hot, cold, wet, and dry all in a matter of hours sometimes - but I wouldn't have it any other way. It's just the being out there that I love."

The freedom and natural surroundings of the job sounded enticing to me and I wanted to know more, but he suddenly announced he was at his exit. I looked around - this was not the usual interstate exit. It was just a wide spot in the road, a gate in the fence line and a two-track that headed off into the hills. We were about thirty miles north of Cheyenne, but this was his exit from civilization. He apologized for leaving me there, and then headed off across country into the hills.

I was alone. It was dark and the land was deserted. There was not a building in sight, nor was there any traffic on the highway. To the east of me I saw a wide expanse of high country grassland stretching off to the horizon. To the west were the foothills of the mountains. I was alone on Interstate 25 with no entrance ramp or turn-off area and a little bit spooked by it all. Every hitchhiker knows - and fears - there may be a time when they are dropped off in the middle of nowhere and stranded. This seemed to be my time. It was 6:00 a.m. and dawn was just breaking. There was no traffic and no place for drivers to turn off even if they could see me.

Then, without warning, as I stood there lost in my isolation, it started to rain. Not a quiet little shower, but a torrential downpour. I was caught off guard, and I desperately tried to cover things up. I tried to put on my little army poncho and cover my backpack, but the more I tried and the more I fought the poncho, the wetter I became. It did not take long before the poncho funneled the rain water right down my back and into my underwear. Within minutes I was soaked.

Then a wonderful thing happened. While standing at the side of the highway in the rain, I looked to the east and saw one of the most beautiful sunrises ever experienced. I was in one of those magical spots in the west where you could see forever. The flat plains stretched out to the east shrouded in clouds and rain all the way to the horizon, but when the sun rose it seemed to push the clouds away and display its full power and brilliance. It rose as a huge ball of fire and cast its warm rays under the rain clouds and brightened the day. To my west the foothills of the Rockies began to glow red in the new warmth of the day. It was still pouring rain where I was, but a brilliant rainbow was created that arched completely across the western sky with a full spectrum of colors and splendor. As I watched this promising spectacle of nature, I knew - even though I was soaked to the skin and alone somewhere in Wyoming with no possible rides in sight - I was going to be okay. I was overcome with emotion and in awe of nature. Although drenched, I was at total peace with the world. Everything I was planning and that had come to pass all seemed to fit into the natural world. And although I should have been uncomfortable and uneasy, I felt a warm glow of sunshine pass through me. As the sun rose in the east and promised another beautiful, hope filled day, I knew God was watching over me. The forces of nature and the forces of God were everywhere, and I was just a small part of the entire picture.

About an hour later, after the rain had stopped and I had dried off, I was picked up by a guy in a pickup who gave me a ride to westbound Interstate 80. But I have always considered that lonely early morning downpour as the turning point in my religious beliefs. That time on the Wyoming roadside was God's test of my faith and trust in Him. Most of all, it was a moment when I realized the wonderful beauty of the Lord's world and its importance to me. The rain, the sunrise, and the warming sunshine all soaked into me never to disappear. I knew there was a God and He must be a good God to have made the earth with all the wonderful things I had witnessed and all the wonderful people I had met.

Over the years I have seen many beautiful, awe in-spiring places. And each of them, in their own way, has made me understand the wonderful and magnificent Supreme Power. Whether you call him God, Allah, Yahweh, Brahman, the Great Father, or any of many names for the Divine Spirit, He has created a fascinat-ing and ever changing world for us to be a part of and experience. I am a believer in the evolution of Earth and all its components, but I also believe there was, and is, a God - the Supreme Creator - who has put all of those evolutionary principles in motion and made us a key part of the world. While many may say we are the masters of God's world, I think it is more important to realize we are just one part of His world. Humans are as much a part of this world as the plants, animals, mountains, streams, and lakes. We are special because we are made in God's image, but since we are part of this world, we have to take care of it and not abuse it. God has given us the intelligence and wisdom to use

Earth to our advantage, but also the ability to know how to stop our abuse of Earth and know we have to preserve His world.

He is constantly presenting us with new challenges – be they the wars and political turmoil of the medieval era, the environmental challenges and powerful changes in society the Industrial Revolution brought on, or our current problems of finding a balance between our need for non-renewable natural resources and our desire to preserve the environment. The beauty of the American West, the Pacific Coast, Northern Michigan, the Smoky Mountains, the Alps, the Irish coastline, or any other natural spot is a great testament to the power of God. How humanity has chosen to live with that beauty and how we have used it to create our society, is the history of the world and it will continue to be the thing upon which history will turn.

Although I have always considered myself a Christian, I believe all religions have more in common than they have differences. All the major religions have some form of heaven or paradise, and you can enter that paradise by living a good life according to the teachings of the faith. You should lead a morally upright life, follow a holy set of rules or commandments, try to build a better community, love your neighbor, live a life of peace, and have faith in the theology of the religion. They all have some special leader, or leaders, that have told us how to live and what we need to do to get to heaven. These are the basic theological ideals of all religions.

As these religions developed, each in its own unique place, these similar ideas became integral to their faith. The theology of Judaism and Christianity fit into the needs, beliefs, and culture of the peoples of the Mediterranean world two millennium ago. The theology of Mohammed fit the needs, beliefs, and culture of the tribal world of the Arabs in the eighth century. Likewise, Hinduism and Buddhism evolved from the social, political and philosophical ideas of the peoples of Asia and the Indian subcontinent. Even the so called "pagan" faiths of the Native American tribes, the central Asian tribes, the Scandinavian and pre-Christian Germanic world all had similar ideas of dominant powers and helped explain the unexplainable world they lived in. Yes, God created humans in his own image, but humans have also created a god to fit into their image and needs.

Throughout the ages, religion has always been used to explain the unexplainable and today's world is no different. When the people of the ancient world could not explain something, they developed religious beliefs to explain the chaos of their world. Today, when we can't make sense of wars and disease, when the political chaos seems impossible to figure out, when we are suffering from personal loss and tragedy, and we are in stress and preparing to die, we need some sort of higher power to ask for help and to give some promise of the future. In this way all religions are the same.

Religious beliefs are a personal thing, requiring an internal inspection of what you believe and what you do not accept. That is not necessarily the same as what a particular church may believe or what a religious leader may teach. Belonging to a church is being part of a community. The church is a group of people with similar religious ideals who want to share those experiences and thoughts. The church provides needed organization and structure. That is good and essential in human society. But the deeper, inner faith in a higher power is much more personal. It requires a personal understanding and acceptance of God and a personal belief and interpretation in the holy writings of a particular theology. And anything that requires an interpretation - whether by an individual or the religion's leadership - can become subject to differences in emphasis, understanding, and the particular goal of the reader. The holy writings of all the major religions have contradictions and vague generalities that can be interpreted many different ways. That is why we have many different religions. A person's beliefs and acceptance of a higher power becomes the baseline of their religious beliefs. And, as a result of that personal belief and faith, religious ideals differ.

While religious beliefs developed in their various regions, they were supported by secular political leaders who saw the advantages of having the religious leadership on their side. European monarchs became more powerful with the blessings of the Pope and support of the local bishop. Similarly, Arab tribal leaders gained power as they gathered support from the Islamic religious leadership. But as the population of the world started expanding and traveling to foreign lands they discovered that not everyone believed the same thing. As these cultures spread, the most powerful was usually the victor in imposing their beliefs - religious and otherwise - on the weaker peoples. The Spanish settlement, colonization, and imposition of Christianity on the natives of Central and South America is a prime example.

America's freedom of religion and the modern shrinking of the world in the twenty-first century have changed all that. Religious ideas and cultures now have daily conflict and overlapping areas of influence. Now we have a vast multitude of religions competing for acceptance by a diverse group of people. The beauty of freedom of religion is we can all worship according to our own conscience and personal beliefs. The problem with that same freedom is that we have to accept others may not agree with our ideas about faith and a higher power. When we cannot accept those personal differences of faith and theology, or the competitiveness which arises because of different beliefs, we have arguments, conflicts, and wars. These differences of opinion can lead to minor inconveniences, especially at a local level - like not being able to have a government-sponsored Nativity scene - or they can lead to much larger problems. Globally, religious differences, and the subsequent failure of others to accept those differences, have led to many of the political and social problems of the world. Most of the current conflicts in the twenty-first century have religious differences as at least one of their causes. It all seems so simple, but is so complicated.

I have always felt my real church is the world around me and the faith I have in a kind, compassionate, and loving God. As many have said before me - heaven is all around, just open your eyes to the beauty of the earth. We must live a life of sound moral judgment, helping our fellow person, and working for peace and understanding among all the peoples of the earth. Those ideals do not fall into any one denomination, and they do not have to be worshiped in a particular building or institution. Civilization has made some spectacular architectural masterpieces to worship in, but sometimes the greatest house of worship can be a lush green forest, a barren desert, the seaside, or the top of a mountain. It can even be on a deserted roadside in the rain. It proved to me God is all around us in everything we see and feel. He has made us smart enough to be able to comprehend His wonderful works. Therein lays the basis of my religious ideology. And I'm convinced I came to that conclusion on that lonely, wet morning in eastern Wyoming.

May 30:

Art got me up at 4:00 AM so he could take me part of the way. He had to go out in the boonies to ride and herd cattle. Sounds like a fantastic job!

My luck seemed to run out (but maybe not!) – Out in the rain. Kinda wanted to take 34 across to Laramie with Art, but I was afraid I'd get stuck in nowhere so I chickened out and took the long way to Cheyenne and around. Guess it worked out OK. Got a ride with a cowboy – really a great guy. Seemed like he led such a quiet, peaceful, hard, but fun life. He seemed to thoroughly enjoy what he was doing and life [in general]. Really cool. Dropped me off 30 miles north of Cheyenne at 6 AM – pouring rain! I spent an hour there and it was one of the best hours of my life. How can I say it except [to say] it was an hour with God. After that hour I knew I was doing the right thing and that my mind was on the right track. Have you ever enjoyed suffering and misery? Not really enjoyed it, but learned so much from it that you knew it wasn't suffering and misery at all – only an education – or even more. I don't know, but I know it was all worth it. I've done a lot of things right and a lot wrong on this trip, but I'd never trade one minute or one step of it. I could do it again tomorrow (with a little less stuff!) I guess I'm kind of a reincarnated pioneer or something, but this land gets to you. You can't see enough of it. You've GOT to climb that hill and see that next bluff. You've gotta go. Being alone seems to have added a lot to this. I almost hated to get picked up – but I knew I had to. I can't say any more about this now – but it's got a hold on me and I know I'll have more to say later. It grabs you and won't let go!

Memorial Day with the Mormons

I made it to Salt Lake City that day. It had been a wild and crazy day and I wanted to talk to my parents to tell them about it. Once I got settled, I called home.

When Dad answered the phone, the operator said, "I have a collect call for anyone from Tom Laughlin." which was my way of saying, "I want to talk." As soon as we were connected Dad said, "You okay?"

"Yeah, I'm fine. Didn't mean to upset you, but I just wanted to talk for a couple minutes. I've had a very interesting day and felt like I wanted to share it with you."

"Great. Glad you called. Go ahead - Mom's on the other phone."

"It was a wild morning. I stayed with a guy in Guernsey, Wyoming, last night. He was just a teenage kid who works as a cowboy rounding up cattle out on the open range. Really cool. Anyways, he had to take me to the highway about 5:00 this morning and I was stuck there for a while. It started to rain and I got drenched. But then there was the most beautiful sunrise I've ever seen. You would have loved it Mom. Anyways, I eventually got picked up and had a couple more rides. But I'm in Salt Lake City now. I'm fine, really - just wanted to share with you a little." I was rambling, but they just let me talk.

"I had a crazy trip across Wyoming. I got picked up by this Marine west of Cheyenne. He had to get back to Camp Pendleton, California by tomorrow or he would be AWOL. He had been driving all night, so he asked me if I would drive while he slept a little. So I drove and he slept in the back seat. It was kinda nice to be driving, but I soon found out his car was a piece of junk. The wheels were out of alignment, there was a hole in the muffler, the steering was loose and worst of all, the brakes were bad." I heard my mother sigh on the other end of the line. "Mom - I know you never would have let me drive it if you were here! I eventually woke the guy up and made him drive. He took me all the way to Salt Lake City, so I'm not complaining too much. But it was a pretty wild ride.

"Have you guys ever been to Utah? It's beautiful!" I gushed. "We came through the Wabash Mountains on the east side of the state and they were spectacular. They seem to rise straight up from the valley floor. I loved the landscapes between Wyoming and Utah - it's really gorgeous land. Then we came out of the mountains and came right down into the Salt Lake Valley. The view was fantastic. I love it.

"I've got a room in a hotel tonight, Mom, so you don't have to worry about me sleeping in the streets or anything like that. I was going to stay in the city park, but it's supposed to rain and the park was already full of people, so I came to the Hotel Stratford instead. It's not fancy - but it's dry and safe."

I was excited and talking about everything. I did not even give my parents a chance to reply.

"The real reason I called though was to tell you about the Mormon Temple and the Tabernacle. I wandered down to Temple Square this evening and stepped into the Tabernacle. The building is beautiful. It's a spectacular setting and there was a service going on, so I quietly took a seat in the back. It was only then that I realized it was Memorial Day."

Dad commented about the holiday, but I kept on talking. "You guys should have heard the choir sing. They sang 'America the Beautiful' and I kept thinking about the prairie and the mountains I had traveled through in the last couple of days. It was so appropriate to where I've been. Then they said a special prayer for all the service members overseas and in particular in Vietnam. All I could think about was Fred, Gary and all our friends who have been over there. I have to admit it choked me up a little.

"I know I've been rambling, but it's really been a great trip so far. Better than I had planned, and I just wanted to say thanks to you guys for letting me do it. So how are things back in Michigan?"

We talked for another ten minutes. I answered my parents' questions, and listened to them talk. They seemed impressed with what I had done and not too anxious for me. I was glad I had called.

After the call I reflected on the last couple of days and thought about everything I had seen and heard. I thought of my reason for traveling west – to attend ROTC boot camp – and on my feelings of patriotism for our nation. Most of all, I thought back to the morning's sunrise and my feeling of being one with God and nature. It had been a special day - I had experienced the beauty of God's natural surroundings at the beginning of the day, and then ended the day in a beautiful manmade sanctuary to that God. The contrast of nature's powerful creation and man's creation was interesting to think about. And behind it all was God's love of the world.

I privately shed some tears of personal gratitude, counted my many blessings, and said a long prayer of thanks. Life was good.

Guernsey, Wyoming to Salt Lake City was over 520 miles. It had been a long day, but I was happy and on schedule.

Journal of May 30 continued:

Had a police check outside Laramie. Wasn't bad but he threatened arrest if he saw me around Rawlins – So I got a ride to Salt Lake. Could have gone all the way to Reno tonite, but the car was in bad shape (no brakes, steering or trans.) and the driver was too! (No sleep) I didn't really mind though, he was quiet and let me think and sleep.

Salt Lake seems nice; think I'll go check it out. (The Stratford Hotel is in a very convenient location – plus only $3.00) – Cashed first traveler's check for $10.00.

Salt Lake is a nice town. Went to the Temple and walked into the Tabernacle to catch the last 10 minutes of a Memorial Day service. (Didn't realize it [was Memorial Day] until later.) Heard the choir – really beautiful. Made me think of Mom. Of all the sights so far, I think she would have liked the choir, Temple, grounds, etc. the best. Was very nice and very inspiring. The beauty of the area and the people makes this a very nice place to see.

Went from Ft. Laramie to Ft. Bridger – then to Salt Lake in a day. Covered the same area it would have taken pioneers about 3 – 4 weeks to cross. S. Western Wyo. is really weird. It has its own type of beauty. Flat, table top buttes, desolation, scrub – and not a tree in sight – almost frightening. Utah is a beautiful state (eastern part anyways). Mountains and canyons. Massive cliffs. Wish I had a super wide angle lens – but my eyes do that and sometimes memory and mental pictures built from what you see are better than the real thing. I don't think my memory of the way into SLC will be anything except beauty and awe and ... wow!

DRIVERS - DAY 4

35. Wheatland – Just N. of Cheyenne = Cowboy in the true sense of the word. Broke horses. The company only had 2-3 vehicles – used horses for everything – loved horses and outdoors – shrugged off what sounded like hard work. Most interesting guy.
- An hour w/ God and water –
36. 2 cowboys into Cheyenne
37. To I-80
38. Past Laramie w/ a guy who had picked up 4 other hikers to Frisco
39. To Salt Lake City = a marine going from Iowa to Monterey, Cal. Without sleep. I drove some – quiet guy. Car was hurtin.
40. Into S.L. City

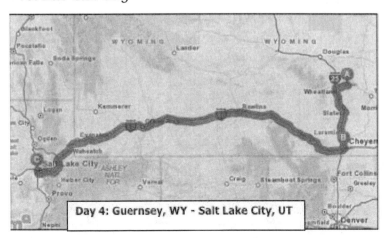

Day 4: Guernsey, WY - Salt Lake City, UT

Across the Desert to Reno

My first ride the next day was with a group of three young people going to San Jose, California to start the hippie life. Their vehicle was a rundown panel van loaded with all their possessions, pets, and other valuables. As we rolled along they were very open and honest – talked about school, drugs, sex, politics, and anything else that came into their minds. As we crossed the Great Salt Lake Desert and traveled into the vastness of Nevada I studied the land and again thought back to the early western emigrants and wondered how they could ever walk across that hot, dry, desolate territory. This was the route the Donner Party took before they became stuck in the Sierra Nevada snows, and it was also the route of thousands of dreamers hoping to strike it rich in the California gold fields. The dreams and hopes of western settlement were all encompassing and the magnet that is California already had a pull on the American psyche.

I dozed off at one point only to wake as we slowly coasted to a stop in the middle of nowhere in Nevada. The van was making terrible noises and we determined the wheel ball bearings were worn out. When help did arrive it was decided to tow the van into the nearest city – Winnemucca – and get the bearings fixed. Since I really did not have much of an alternative other than stand on the roadside by myself, I decided to ride to Winnemucca with the rest of the folks. However, within a couple of miles the bearings were in such bad shape and so worn down the wheels started smoking. When we stopped the wheel assembly burst into flames. The van owner ran around trying to figure out what to do. I stayed out of the way and, as I pondered all the highly inflammable materials I had seen in the van, realized this could quickly degrade into a very dangerous situation. Luckily the fire was put out within a couple of minutes without spreading. Upon further discussion, it was decided the van had to be left at the roadside to be picked up later. Now we were all stranded.

At that point I chose to leave my happy little group of western wanderers and stuck my thumb out to get another ride. Within a few minutes I was picked up by two members of the Air Force who took me the rest of the way to Reno, which had been my destination for the day.

May 31:

Walked out to the xway and had a long wait. Finally got picked up by 2 guys and a girl from Brigham Young going to San Jose. [They were] driving a panel truck loaded to the limit. Real good kids and we had a lot of fun until about ½ way across Nevada. The truck broke down! We (I) waited about an hour while one guy went into Winnemucca to get help. Men pulled us about 2 mi. and the rear wheel caught on fire! Took about 10 - 15 min. of frantic running around and many near suicide attempts to put it out. I stayed out of there. Left them 'cause they were going to be all night. Got a ride w/2 Air Force men. These guys were really funny. They had all kinds of troubles too and were making a 12 hour ride into an 18 hr. one. Good guys.

I have always enjoyed watching people. It is interesting to look at people in a crowded place and see the variety of clothes, cultural influences, desires and tastes. While you cannot know people just by looking at what they are wearing, or what they are doing, it is fun to speculate. It is a great way to understand the differences in the world. I was fascinated with the variety of people I met throughout my journey west, but it was never more true than in the casinos of Reno, Nevada. In 1971, casino gambling was legal only in Nevada and Atlantic City, New Jersey, so visiting the casinos was something special for a Michigan boy. Casinos were famous for bringing in all sorts of people and to a naïve young man like myself, who had never been in a casino before, it was fun to watch people and learn many of my personally held stereotypes were true – but many were false. I spent as much time walking around and looking at people as I did gambling. Upon returning to the University of Michigan the following fall I wrote an assignment for a composition class about the people in Reno. I described them in a myriad of ways: "oblivious to the action around them," "expressing little emotion," or "tense and excited...squealing with excitement," "calm and reassured." "Some were thrilled, noisy, uneasy, and bold, while others were confident, quiet, patient, and relaxed."

As I traveled west, I met people with money and people who were desperate for jobs. There were people brimming with confidence and others who kept looking over their shoulder for the next bad thing to happen. I met bankers, beggars, students, grandparents, farmers, teachers, soldiers, and peaceniks. There were all sorts of people with all sorts of opinions and while I did not agree with all of them, I made it a point to not disagree too strongly and to respect what they had to say. I tried to listen to every viewpoint and learned that every situation - be it a war, economy, business, or occupation - had good and bad points. Every person had a different perspective and an honest belief their ideas were right. I learned it was best to listen and explore all the perspectives and to look at both sides before forming an opinion. The diversity of people and their thoughts were what made things interesting.

Hitchhiking across the country was a bit like gambling. You needed steely nerves, had to study people, and sometimes just had to lay it out there and trust fate. I had always liked to play penny ante poker with friends, but had never been to a casino or gambled for more than a couple of dollars. I was excited to try my luck, but since I did not have much money I wasn't going to play any of the high stakes games. I played Black Jack and got lucky, so I stayed there most of the night. My dealer for much of the evening was a shapely blond twenty-four year old woman who had just finished her first year as an elementary teacher and was working as a dealer for her summer job. Initially I sat at her table because of her good looks, but as the evening wore on I seemed to win whenever she was dealing. I would play Black Jack when she was dealing, then when the dealers rotated and she took a break, I would walk around looking at people. When she returned, I would go back to her table. She was easy to talk to and we soon discovered similarities talking about education, teaching, and her first year experiences. We got to know each other in a short time.

By 2:00 a.m. fewer and fewer people were playing at her table, which was fine with me since I was winning. I wasn't making huge bets, but I managed to get about $90 ahead before my luck started to turn. Then, contrary to the usual stereotype of casino workers being cold-hearted people who want to take your money, my cute school teacher dealer showed her humane side. After a couple of losing hands she took the cards and refused to deal me another hand. When I asked her why, she quietly said, "You're ahead right now. Go home. I don't want you to lose the little bit you have gained. You can use that money for the rest of your trip." I realized she was right. I had been caught up in the gambling and casino atmosphere. It was time for me to go home. I also realized how thoughtful and personal my dealer had become – not what I expected. That made my casino visit much more satisfying.

On this day I traveled 500 miles getting to Reno and was over 2000 miles from home. I loved the beauty and stark vastness of the great American west, but was getting ready for civilization and some company. I have always enjoyed traveling and have never regretted taking this trip by myself, but I also wondered how it would have been different if I had a companion to share it with.

Journal of May 31 continued:

[In Reno] I got a cheap room in the Morris Hotel. Not bad for me. Then I hit the tables. Stayed mostly at "Harrah's", but saw some others. 21 was my game. Took in $18.00 to lose – Brought home $27.00 in winnings! Could have had more ($35) but I had a lot of fun and the little I did win paid for my trip out here. Had some bad times – like betting my last buck and getting ready to go home – only to start winning. But it was worth it. Guess that casino was just as I imagined it would be. People in them are amazing – really fascinating. Old grannys playing 2 or 3 slot machines at once and not even waiting to see if they'd won before the next coin went in. $100.00 bills being flashed around. Mothers playing 21 who didn't know what an ace counted! The epitome of a dumb blonde cocktail waitress – the slim silent, long fingered dealers – and Jerry (the floor walker, checker, whatever) in his dark glasses, flashy suit, just as you'd imagine in a casino, who broke down into a really decent sounding guy when you talked to him (He hated gambling – had a teacher's certificate –

*same as my dealer – but got more money and enjoyed
the work and people at Harrah's.)*

*Utah is a fantastic state. The Salt Lake Desert
was great – amazingly flat w/nothing there, not even the
little scrub bushes in places. It's hypnotizing. It was
over 40 miles to the mts. on the other side but they
looked like they were about 2 – 4 blocks away! It didn't
seem like you moved at all 'cause you'd look out and see
the same thing you did 5 min. before. And to think the
Donners walked over that for 6 days!*

*Nevada was so alone! There is nothing in Nevada
(not even the nothing of the Desert!) Rolling hills and
valleys and mountains. The starkness of the land is
awe inspiring. The most fascinating thing though, I
think, was the hugeness of the sky and the different
types of weather you could see at one time in one sky.
One place, for ex. – there were huge dark storm clouds
on the right and left sides of the road, but we never got
wet and were in a sunny zone all along. Meanwhile in
the same sky, you could see a place where it was per-
fectly clear, or watch clouds build up, etc. It is hard to
explain but something to see.*

DRIVERS - DAY 5

*41. 3 Kids from Brigham Young U. going home to San
Jose. Real nice and fun. Truck broke down in middle of
Nevada (25 mi. E. of Winnimucka)*

42. To Reno = 2 guys in the Air Force going back to Cal. From Utah – funny & nice.

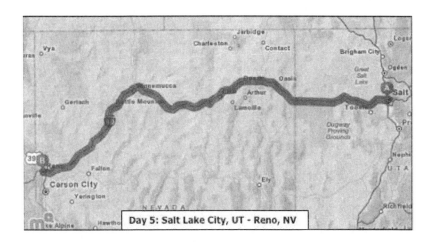

Day 5: Salt Lake City, UT - Reno, NV

California or Bust

I planned on going over the Sierra Nevada Mountains to Yosemite National Park and spending a day there before going to San Francisco, but nature had other plans. I awoke to a cold rainy day and decided to stay in the casinos until the rain stopped. What a mistake. I proceeded to lose most of the winnings from the night before. I did stop before losing everything though, so I felt okay because I had stayed in Reno and managed to break even. It gave me an opportunity to assess my finances for the trip and an appreciation of how cheaply I had crossed the continent.

Over the course of six days I had only spent a little over $22.00. That still amazes me, and I know how little was spent on food or lodging during the trip. Typically, I only had one meal a day, and that was a hamburger and fries. I might have a candy bar and a soda, but that was about it. Three of the five overnights cost me a total of fifty cents and the most expensive hotel room, in Reno, was $8.00 for the night. That still makes me laugh.

As my ride progressed west out of Reno, we climbed into the Sierra Nevada Mountains. These were the same ranges and peaks that had stopped the Donner Party back in the 1840's and forced them to resort to cannibalism to survive. Now the pass was part of Interstate 80 and another small obstacle on my way to San Francisco. Donner Pass – the top of the Sierra Nevada Range – was still an area of vast wilderness and could be dangerous if you were lost and alone. There was still snow at the top in June and I imagined what it must have been like to be snowed in with few provisions and nothing to save you. Then I sat back and enjoyed the comfort of my ride.

I arrived at Aunt Becky's in the afternoon on June 1, 1971. My ride from Reno took me all the way to the eastern side of San Francisco Bay. From there I got a ride to Mill Valley with a school teacher and, although he offered to take me up the hill to Aunt Becky's, I chose to get out and walk the last mile to her house. It seemed very symbolic to walk. I had hitchhiked over 2500 miles with no real mishaps. I could not have asked for more. Aunt Becky and Uncle Bob were overjoyed to see me and for the next week I enjoyed their company and hospitality. But as comfortable as I was in their house, I kept going back to the trip and kept preparing to get back on the road again.

June 1 (in car):

So today (6/1) may be my last day out. I hate to see it end, and to go by Yosemite, but I think I will. From the reports I got its bad weather up there. If I go to Beck's now I think she, or Chris, or Lee, will bring me back to Yosemite. I sure hope so. But I don't want it to end.

It has been too good probably. But there will be other times and other places and I know how and what to do and take. So I'll be ready and my pack will always be on 24 hr. alert. Cuz once you've been there – you know and love the world and to know and love the world is to know and love life.

Well, I was a victim of circumstances, Mother Nature, and my own stupidity. Since it was raining this morning I postponed Yosemite. And to waste time until the rain stopped I went back to Harrah's. What a dummy. I should have known better. I make matters worse; I was ahead for a while and didn't have the brains to quit! So instead of leaving Reno $27 ahead I'm only $17 ahead. Of course that means I came out west for about $4 or $5, which isn't bad! Course it would be nice to say I made 4 –5 dollars on the way out. Only I played w/ Harrah's money anyways.

So now I'm on my final leg to Mill Valley. Well I guess I'm ready for a little civilization – but not too much!

"I'd rather wake up in the middle of nowhere than in any city on earth" – Steve McQueen

I made it – kinda wish I'd gotten lost or something – but I'm glad I'm here.

So I guess it's over – kinda. I loved every minute of it and every bit of it was great. But maybe it's not over, but only the beginning. I don't know – It will take time and thought to know what I've gained and learned. So I guess it has just begun.

Appendix:
Under 6/1 – Forgot to mention my impressions of the Sierras. Mostly it wasn't the mountains but the nature of the mts. that was so fascinating. June 1 and there was a foot of snow in the side of the road and it had snowed the night before. The Donners couldn't make it in 1846 and ended up eating each other. In 1971 man still has a hard time coping w/Mother Nature and often gets snowed in up there!

As I reread the last journal entry I realized how far off target Dad's prediction was that "this will get the travel bug out of his system." Obviously, I wanted more traveling, and was ready to go again. I still had lots of traveling and many miles to go before my summer adventure was complete, but I was already starting to see the affect it would have on me. *Cuz once you've been there – you know and love the world and to know and love the world is to know and love life.*

On the last few pages of the little notebook that was my journal I kept a log of drivers. Forty-five different people with forty-five different personalities and stories. Each of them affected me in some way, even the ones that only gave me a ride for a couple of miles. It does seem significant, looking back on the list, that I only give the names of two particular drivers - Joe the truck driver in Illinois and Art Kennedy in Guernsey, Wyoming. Most were just nameless people who I talked to and learned from, but who never got personal enough for us to exchange names. That was one of the strange things about hitchhiking - you got close to a person and discussed a lot of interesting topics, but never got too close. It's hard to imagine that today.

DRIVERS - DAY 6

43. Reno to N. of Mill Valley = guy going to Santa Rosa – nice guy, but quiet.

44 – 45. Guys going S. to get me near Mill Valley

- Final 2 mi – me! Wanted to walk it – just to walk it I guess. But I'm there and feel great.

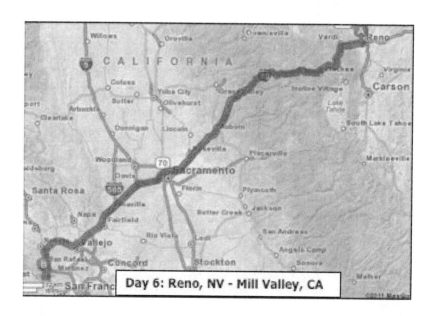

Day 6: Reno, NV - Mill Valley, CA

San Francisco

Aunt Becky and Uncle Bob Matson were always the mystery family of the Green clan. Not that they did anything mysterious – Uncle Bob had a good job with the Chevron Corporation – but they were the part of the family that did not live in Michigan and we did not visit regularly. They had lived in Washington D.C. and the San Francisco area for years and rarely came back to Michigan. When they did come back, it was always a big deal and cause for a Green family reunion. In the summer of 1970 they visited Michigan, and it was then that Aunt Becky remarked I was welcome to visit any time. Her invitation became much more important when I started organizing my summer plans for 1971 and was the key factor in my being able to attend Fort Lewis. When I asked if I could visit, Aunt Becky was more than happy to roll out the red carpet and to make my stay memorable.

It was wonderful to come into their home and have a bedroom to myself, to shower and clean up, and have as much food as I wanted. After six days on the road I appreciated the order and cleanliness of their home. Aunt Becky and Uncle Bob's house was situated in the foothills overlooking the northern end of San Francisco Bay and we would sit on the deck at night and watch the lights come on in Sausalito and San Francisco. The entire area was enchanting. As soon as I was settled, I called home and had a long conversation with Mom and Dad, then sat down to update my journal. I shared my journal and stories with Aunt Becky, who was an eager and empathetic listener. She mothered me, but was also a great companion to share ideas with.

My cousins Chris, a year older, and Aletha, two years younger than me, were more than happy to show me around and I soon had expeditions of the Bay Area planned with the family. After a day of relaxing, calling home, and catching up on things, I was able to enjoy the beauty of the San Francisco Bay area. Becky took me to her favorite spots – Muir Redwood National Monument, the beach, and into San Francisco. The visit to Muir Woods was very impressive as the giant redwoods and the quiet solitude of the park created a wonderful spot to appreciate the beauty of nature and the magnificence of the trees.

The highlight of the stay was when Chris, Aletha, and I went to Yosemite National Park for two days of hiking and enjoying the scenery. The Yosemite Valley, Half Dome, El Capitan, and the Merced River Valley were beautiful and majestic, but it was the little things that were magical; the serenity of the forest floor contrasted with the thundering power of the waterfalls; the bright blue sky accentuated the harsh cold of the granite cliffs; the gentle ache in your limbs that came after walking and climbing all day. I fondly remember curling up in my sleeping bag at 8000 feet elevation and seeing a magnificent canopy of stars before dropping off to a sound, restful sleep.

Aunt Becky also gave me opportunities to explore the city by myself, so one day I drove into San Francisco and wandered around. Since this was the era of the hippies, I went to the Haight-Ashbury area to see what all the fuss of San Francisco free love was about. Walking through the famous neighborhood where "peace," "love," and "free your mind" were common expressions, I found young men and women fitting the stereotype of hippies - long hair, cheap tie-dyed clothes and sandals, smoking marijuana and looking for something else in their life. I also found they were looking at the world passing by as much as the world was looking at them.

Haight-Ashbury was a poor, run-down area with a lot of young people who looked more like homeless, desperate, hung over, and drugged out, down and out bums than the exotic, fun-loving, exciting place the media and reputation had made it out to be. The youth counterculture - the hippies - wanted us to believe they represented a new life of independence, freedom, and unrestrained love and peace among people. But they had as many needs, frustrations, and desires for material success as anyone else. Every generation has rebelled against their elders - theirs was just more visible to the world than many others had been. They had freedom and independence, but it also seemed selfish and way too chaotic for me. I loved my freedom on the road, but I wanted more order and structure in my world. Although I could empathize with their ideas and desires, I could not live that lifestyle.

After visiting Haight-Ashbury I drove to Golden Gate Park and stopped at the ocean to watch a group of sea lions swimming and sunning at the entrance to San Francisco Bay. I found a large flat rock and sat down, watched the sea lions, and spent time reflecting on a beautiful day. While sitting there a young man came up and casually sat on a nearby rock. We struck up an innocent conversation about the sea lions, the weather, and other superficial matters. Of course he asked where I was from, which led to a lengthy explanation of how I had hitchhiked across the country and some of my experiences. He was very interested, asked lots of questions, and seemed like a very nice new friend. It was getting late, so I quietly stated I had to go.

"Well, before you go, why don't we slip back behind the rocks for a quickie?" he calmly asked.

I was taken off guard and way too naïve to understand the significance of what he was asking and said, "What?"

"Yeah, we could go back there and no one would see us. I'll gladly pay you if you let me."

His polite casualness seemed reassuring but I wasn't interested. Then I came to my senses and realized I was being propositioned by a gay man.

"Huh - No thanks. I'm not interested in anything like that."

"OK - but I had to ask." and he nonchalantly excused himself and walked away. I did not see him again.

The visit to Haight-Ashbury and the proposition on the rocks sent me back to Aunt Becky's with a new realization of who I was and where my values were. I did not have any objection to the hippie lifestyle or their choices of drugs, sex, and living freely, but I personally could not live that life. While I always wanted to live freely and make my own decisions, I liked order too much to ever live that way. Family, work, and a stable lifestyle were very important. I did not like losing control of that and felt it was being sacrificed by the Haight-Ashbury, hippie lifestyle.

The experience with the young gay at the rocks of Golden Gate had an even greater influence. Up to that point in my life I had never met an openly gay person. In the Sixties - at least in eastern Michigan - you did not openly proclaim homosexual preferences for fear of the social discrimination and ramifications that would occur. San Francisco already had a reputation for a large gay and lesbian community, but I had not thought about it before being asked by the young man at the park. As he walked away, I realized I had absolutely no interest in his lifestyle either. However, I was very impressed with this young man's interest in my trip, his politeness, and his overall appearance. He wasn't a perverted, twisted, sick personality – he was a quiet young man who had different sexual preferences than me. While I did not agree with his sexual choices, he had not tried to force anything on me and had accepted my decision. Those choices were his to make and not mine to try to influence. His life was probably a lot harder than mine when it came to making lasting friends and living a normal life. Both of these experiences showed me how sheltered my life had been and how naïve I was, even at twenty-one years old.

Aunt Becky was a great listener and always had time for me. We had many in depth conversations during the two weeks I stayed with her. We talked frequently about family and how important it was in her life and mine. She wanted me to tell her all about the trip, my impressions, thoughts, and dreams. It became an easy form of therapy to tell her everything on my mind. We talked about history, culture, current events, and life in general. My memories of the stay were one of comfort and a feeling of family needed at that point of the summer.

Strange Days in Northern California

After a wonderful rest and recuperation at Aunt Becky's it was time to get back on the road. I had to hitchhike the remaining thousand miles to Fort Lewis, Washington and I wanted plenty of time to get there. So, on Sunday afternoon, June 13, 1971, I again picked up my little backpack and Aunt Becky took me out to California State Route One where I stuck out my thumb and asked for rides.

Route One is one of the most famous highways in the world, known for its beautiful panoramic views of the Pacific as it winds along the coastline. Most people recognize it for the Big Sur area south of San Francisco, but the northern part is just as scenic. The ocean side cliffs drop off to fantastic beaches, accented by huge monolithic rock formations that break up the shoreline. To the east of the two-lane road are the foothills of the coastal mountains and beautiful green forests. It is an area of small farms, coastal villages, and a much more laid back lifestyle than the rest of California. It's also an area of large-scale lumbering, saw mills, and huge lumber trucks speeding down the road with little concern for hitchhikers or anyone.

The Pacific, like most of the other natural wonders I had seen on the trip, fascinated me. It was powerful yet peaceful, roaring yet serene, limiting yet limitless. It was a barrier to my travels, but it was also a guide for me to follow north. Again, I wanted to become completely involved in the forces of nature it represented. No matter how many times I looked, the Pacific always seemed different and represented something new to me.

Hitchhiking up scenic Route One differed from my earlier hitchhiking experiences. It became a greater test of patience and persistence than the first part of my summer. When I was hitching from Michigan to California I had spent most of my time on interstate highways. Now, for the first couple days of my trip north, I was traveling on two lane state roads with much less traffic. Many of the cars whizzing past were local drivers going short distances and had no interest in picking someone up for only a two or three mile trip. For the first time in the summer I thought I may have taken the wrong route and might have to break down and get some sort of commercial transportation.

Northern California seemed to have a different attitude about hitchhikers. I met some wonderfully open and trusting people who were a pleasure to talk to. Many of the drivers were young and said they had hitchhiked themselves. Often there were two or three other hitchhikers picked up by the same driver. But I also had my first real experiences with drivers who displayed hostility and dislike of hitchhikers. I was given the finger many times during that phase of the trip, had things thrown at me out of windows, and worst of all, attempts by massive logging trucks to run me off the road. More than once I dove into the ditch as a logging truck swerved onto the shoulder where I was standing. I do not know if they really wanted to hit me, or just give me a scare, but I wasn't going to take any chances. However, the scenery was spectacular, the weather was fine, and I had scheduled an extra day into my trip calculations, so I figured it would be okay if I could remain cautious and patient.

My first day back on the road resulted in only 150 miles to MacKerricher State Park along the Pacific coast. I stopped at Fort Ross - a reconstructed Russian fort just north of San Francisco. I could not pass up an historical park, especially one as unique as Fort Ross, which had been a Russian fur trading post in the early 19th century and was the furthest extent of Russian attempts to colonize the western coast of North America. The small reconstructed wooden Russian Orthodox Church, with its onion domed architecture looked very out of place on the western coastline, but it was easy to imagine the profitable fur trade along the Pacific coast. But with American migration west and more American involvement in the California area, the little Russian settlement was too exposed, and too costly to protect. The Russians abandoned the fort in the 1840s. It was an interesting stop to imagine such an isolated colony and what their life must have been like.

Mendocino was my goal for the day and I made it past there and enjoyed the state park and the beach. I shared my little poncho with two other hikers I met on the road thinking it was going to rain, but it cleared up and turned into a pleasant night. It felt good to get back on the road and feel the rush of independence as I made my way north. I did not anticipate this segment of the trip would be much different than the first part. Boy was I wrong.

June 14

Well – it's been just over 2 weeks since I wrote last. There has been a lot done in those 2 wks – lots that I should have written about before – but you don't feel like writing things down when you're in a nice cozy house, etc.

So I'm on the road again. Started about 2:00 yesterday & had pretty good luck – got as far as I planned (Ft. Bragg). Got off today about 10:00 and have gone about 5 miles. I'm on Route 1 by the coast (for over an hour now!) but I'll get a ride soon – so I may seem rather choppy.

I may seem choppy anyways as my mind wanders a bit back and forth between current impressions to thoughts and impressions of the last 2 weeks. There has been so much going through my head and it is so hard to put it all into words, but I have to – for my own sanity if nothing else!

Think I'll walk on – flies a bit thick here – but the view is nice and the large hawks (possibly Golden Eagles) are impressive.

The Pacific – Melville called it "the heart of the world" – how true. The pulsating, beating, pounding, consistent, eternal, roaring, peaceful, forceful heart of the world. It's hypnotizing and you want to see the other side. So foggy and hazy and yet so clear – so full of life and so life giving. Is this the edge of the world? Is this the end of the world or the beginning. Each wave looks the same, and yet each wave looks different! The Pacific – it forms a limit for my journey – but not an end. Like a fence you follow it along, running parallel to it looking for an opening or a gate – but you can't find it – 'cuz it's the ocean!

See the problem w/ Calif. Is that there are too many hitch-hikers & too few people that will pick them up. Where I figured Cal. would be the best state to thumb in, it is actually the worst. Reason why? Well, the way I see it is because only people of the same generation will pick up someone of that age group. In other words – I haven't had, and probably won't have – a ride w/an older person, businessman, truckers, etc. And all the other thumbers I've seen or met out here it has been the same way. In Mich. and the rest of the Midwest anyone will pick you up if they feel like it, but from S. Lake on I have felt, and become convinced, that the older generation passes up younger generation hitch-hikers and younger generation picks them up. Consequently you get rides w/one driver and 2 or 3 other thumbers – which is a real drag – all you meet are other h-hikers. Also – you get stuck north of Westport, Cal. w/nothing but a nice sunburn to show for it!

DRIVERS - DAY 1 NORTHBOUND

1. *Mill Valley - Stinson Beach:* Guy & girls going to beach - also had another hitchhiker

2. *S. Beach - 1/116 junction - quiet guy. Also another h-hiker.*

3. *to Ft. Ross - girl in van w/4 other h-hikers in rear-end - weird - like a bus for h-hikers*

4. *to Stewerts Pt. - guy w/2 other hikers*

5. *"travelin man": I met on one of the earlier rides. got a ride w/the guys he was w/. The hiker was strange, quiet, said he'd been on the road 5 mts. from N.Y. and going all over - rode w/Cole & Ron - real good guys up to MacKerricher St. Pk. N. of Fort Bragg - shared my tent/lean-to w/them since it looked like rain - but it didn't.*

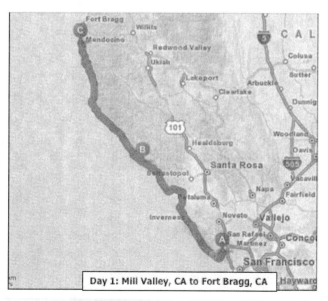

Day 1: Mill Valley, CA to Fort Bragg, CA

Westport and the Child

My father grew up in the small village of Horton, Michigan, so any time I found myself in a small town I thought back to that little crossroads. Westport, California, with a population of 340, was just such a place. It was less than a mile from the southern to the northern edge of town. In later writings I described it as "one gas station, one restaurant, a grocery store/gift shop, a few cottages, and a nice beach." It was a spectacular location, perched on the edge of steep cliffs dropping down to a fantastic beach and unlimited ocean views. It appeared to be one of those small towns that survived because of neighboring farms, some fishing, and a fair share of summer tourist cottages. When I was there it was a quiet little spot in the road to slow down and enjoy the scenery. I do not imagine it is much different today. This would be where I would spend most of my day on June fifteenth.

I walked through the village along Route One until I found a wide spot north of town suitable for a car to pull over. I spent the next four hours waiting for a ride. There was very little traffic so I had plenty of time to write in my journal, daydream, and just watch the ocean beat against the rocks at the bottom of the cliff. As I looked at the Pacific across the street from me, I noticed a unique rock formation.

From where I was standing, it appeared to have the shape of a young man with his arm out trying to hitch a ride. He had been in Westport so long he became petrified with his thumb out. I was determined not to stay in Westport that long.

The Petrified Hitchhiker of Westport

Upon returning to college in August, I had many stories and impressions of the trip to talk about with roommates and friends. That fall semester I took a writing composition class that applied toward my English major. During class, I wrote a number of papers for that class about different experiences of the summer. One in particular was entitled "A Child" about a young boy in Westport. I must have liked the paper - or at least the grade - because I have saved it throughout all these years. It still seems to sum up the memories of that long day spent in a sleepy little seaside village by the Pacific. I will quote some of those impressions here:

> ...I hadn't planned on stopping in Westport. I hadn't planned on stopping anywhere, specifically, just wherever I happened to be dropped off. So I ended up in a small town next to the sea that appeared to have very little to offer me. I was tired and becoming slightly depressed. I hadn't planned on it taking me over two and one-half hours to go from Mendocino to Westport. The coast was magnificent and I was happy to have seen it, but I was ready to move on up the road and see something new.

> "Hello mister! Where're ya goin'?"

> The boy was big for his ten years and very talkative...The boy was the epitome of an adventure-some boy with his fishing pole over his shoulder, his bare feet, and his confident smile. To accompany the smile were his eyes; big, brown, and shining in the sunlight. I had only gone a few hundred yards when I met him, and his radi-

ance and life immediately cheered me
from my depression.

"I'm going to Seattle, Washington."

"Geeee... Is that farther than Eureka?
Where are you from?"

"I'm from Michigan. Do you know where
that is?"

"That's in the United States isn't it?"

"Yep, it's way on the other side of the
country - over 2000 miles away."

"Wow... You didn't walk all that way did
ya?"

"No, I got rides from people on the road."

"Why did you do that mister?"

"That's a good question. I guess because I
like to meet people and see different places."

Just as suddenly as he popped up he was
gone, running down the road with his little brother behind him. Running with that
carefree, limitless energy of the very
young. The farther away he ran, the more
I thought of our conversation. He had
been the first person, besides my drivers,
to talk to me on that day. This child had

been innocent and trusting where other
people had been doubting and suspicious.
He did not have fear. He never hesitated
to be friendly and anxiously pried for answers.

...I saw the boy a few minutes later. I had
walked to the other side of town (an easy
task) and was standing on the roadside
overlooking the ocean. I was entranced by
the sea, its beauty, its peace, and its
power. Off shore were numerous jagged
and precarious boulders that took the full
force of the breakers and shattered them
into fine spray. Below me was a steep,
rugged cliff that presented a barrier between man and water. The beach seemed
to be a transition between these two
scenes of violent action. It lay between the
two dominating features - the rocks and
the cliffs - quiet, smooth, accepting the
power of the waves, yielding to erosion only to be built up in another location.
Suddenly the boy appeared on this scene
in all his innocence. He was alone with
the sand and the water and he loved it.
He ran in the sand, he dodged the waves,
he squealed when hit by the spray, he
waded, and he swam. Than as quickly as
he appeared, he was gone. Gone to find
some other amusement to absorb some of
his energy. He was gone from the beach,
and with him the human touch, his primi-
tive junction with nature, was gone. The

waves and the sand were alone again under the overlooking cliffs.

It was another four hours before I got a
ride out of Westport, and I was glad when
I did. I had stared at that sea and beach
until my eyes burned and I had grown
weary of the entire journey. That day, in
which I only covered forty miles in eight
hours, seemed like the low point of my
trip. Looking at it in retrospect, however, I
see it was only my first impression that
labeled that day as a failure, and that, in
reality, Westport, California, is the place I
think of most and learned the most from.

The purity and trust of the boy were the
most important factors. A warm smile, a
beaming face, a welcome hand, and a gentle acknowledgement are what every
stranger wants to find. His curiosity and
boldness showed his naiveté', but also his
youthful ambition. His antics on the
beach displayed his energetic, carefree life
with   nature. He was the personification
of the innocence and simplicity of childhood so sought after and so easily lost.
He was natural and daring, and free from
the worries of the world. He was a child.

I wrote that paper forty years ago, but the emo-
tions and reactions expressed in it still ring so true,
there is not much more to say.

June 15:

"Where you goin?" he said. Does it really matter?
"No room, sorry!"
"Can you squeeze in there?"
"Just throw it on top – don't worry!"
"Hi mister. How do you get around? Wow – 3000 miles! How far is that anyways?"
"That sure is beautiful country up there son – hope you have a good trip."
It's so easy to tell people, just by the first thing they say. People are a rare breed I guess.
Westport is kind of a neat little town. Pop. 340, elev. 150'. The Horton of the Pacific. The shoreline along here is fantastic – beyond description, but not beyond memory.

Talking to people on the road is so easy – not necessarily so when riding, but people walking or pedaling by are almost always free for a couple of questions – and you can tell a lot w/ a few silly questions. Easiest way is to ask about your route – even though you know it better than they do. Or just a "How ya doin'?" can get interesting results. People sure are funny!

The "Petrified Hitchhiker of Westport, Cal. He's a fellow who was thumbing South on Route 1 and only got as far as Westport! I saw him and sympathized w/ him as he stood there. He must have gone down to the ocean to cool his feet because that's where he is now. A huge granite hitch-hiker kneeling on the beach, still with his thumb out hoping still for a ride. I might join him before

119

the day is out! I have been in Westport (or as far north as I could walk in the last half hour) for about 2 hrs now. I've gone about 16 mi. in 5 hours! I could almost walk that fast! I guess today was just suppose to be my day of no rides. After the rides I got coming out I had to expect a day like today. After all, it is Monday! Guess it's OK – I knew I picked a scenic, but thinly traveled route. And I think it has been worth it. Look at all the writing I got done and caught up on! Oh well – if my back and arms hold up another 5-6 miles... Like the little kid said, "You going to walk to Seattle?" Ya kid!

Eureka is a Good Name for It

I eventually did get a ride out of Westport, but the strange events of the day were only starting. As a matter of fact, the next three days went by so fast, and with such crazy events I did not get to write in my journal until June eighteenth.

I was picked up outside of Westport by a couple in their mid-twenties who would take me north for the next hour or so. They were packed into a small Nissan Datsun sedan, and apparently coming from the beach, since both the man and woman were still in their swimming suits. The young man driving was pleasant looking and friendly, but I must admit my attention was more focused on the shapely young lady in the passenger seat, since she was wearing a very skimpy string bikini.

"If you're not afraid of dogs, you can squeeze in the back," the beauty said as they pulled up next to me. I love dogs so I did not think it would be a problem, until I looked in the back and saw a large, fully grown German shepherd. Since they were the first car to stop in over four hours, I was not going to let the chance go by, even if I did have to contend with the dog for space. "He's really very friendly! He won't hurt you"

I squeezed in next to the dog, who took up about two-thirds of the space in the small back seat. I ended up with my knees jammed up into my chest and my backpack in my lap. It was difficult to sit that way, but I made myself as comfortable as I could. The couple was very nice and quickly made me relaxed by asking the normal questions of "Where are you going?" "Where have you been?" "You're going to Fort Lewis for ROTC? What's that going to be like?" Since I had been asked those same questions many times during the summer, I answered them with ease.

But this was not going to be a normal ride. After about fifteen minutes of driving along a twisty two lane road, through a spectacular redwood forest, the driver pulled out a joint and lit up. "You don't mind do you?" he asked as he passed the joint to his girlfriend.

"No, not at all," I said. I had learned earlier in the trip it really did not matter if I did have a concern. If I wanted to continue riding I had better just agree. I did decide I would not participate though, since it might be good for someone to watch the road.

No sooner had I accepted that my driver and his girlfriend were not going to get too stoned when the lovely young lady decided it was time for her to get out of her bikini. I looked up and saw her untie the bikini string, drop the top in her lap, and very slowly and casually pull on a tee shirt. She then started wiggling around and pulled on her blue jeans. I tried to casually move around a little bit so I could get a better view of what she was doing, but to no avail. I was seated directly behind her, with a pack in my lap and a huge German shepherd panting heavily next to me, so it was impossible for me to move or see anything. I'm sure my eyes must have gotten bigger though, because when I looked at the rear view mirror the driver was looking at me and quietly laughing at my reaction. I tried to stay cool, but I'm sure my eyes and facial expression gave me away. Not a word was said by any of us for a few minutes as I'm sure my exhibitionist friend was having a good little laugh at my expense.

They dropped me off about ten miles from Eureka, California, without any further excitement and I soon had another ride into Eureka. My plan was to spend the night at the state park just outside of town. While waiting for my next ride, an old clunker of a car stopped with a rather disreputable looking guy inside who leaned out the window and asked if I needed a ride. Hitchhiking all those miles had created a sixth sense about potential drivers and for some reason there was something about this guy I did not like.

"Where you from?" he asked.

"Michigan - I'm on my way up to Fort Lewis, Washington."

"Wow - all the way from Michigan. I'll bet you have some stories to tell."

"Yeah - I've had an interesting trip," I said as I tried to further measure him up and see what his angle was without disclosing many details about myself.

"Hey - I've got a friend you should meet. He's a writer - lives in Florida - and he's writing a book about kids like you. His book is going to be about traveling across America. Climb in and I'll hook you up with him. I think it would be great. Are you interested?"

I still did not have a good feeling about this one, and luckily I had the perfect excuse. "Sounds cool, but I really can't. I've got to be at Fort Lewis in two days to start Boot Camp. I can't be AWOL ya know."

"OK - But I think you're missing out on a good deal." And with that he left.

I'm not sure why I chose to climb into one driver's car and not another, but I have always felt my instincts were good. Being young and naive was often beneficial in meeting people, but I still believe this guy could have been dangerous. The requirement to be in Fort Lewis was a good excuse, so I never seriously considered his offer. Now I realize how fortunate I was. Soon afterwards Kent picked me up and one of the more interesting stops of the trip proceeded to take place.

There were some things deliberately left out of my journal because I knew Mom and Dad would be reading it when I got home. The evening with Kent was just such an event. He was a thin, intelligent looking young man in his early twenties driving a Volkswagen bus. There was something about him that put me at ease and made me trust him.

"Where you headed?" He asked when he pulled over.

"Up to the state park for the night."

While driving through town Kent noted the weather changing and said, "If you want, you can stay at my place. You can sleep in the back of the van."

"That would be great, if you don't mind."

"It's fine. I live about ten miles east of here in the woods. I've got a homestead back on some federal land I'm settling."

We drove out of town to what he called his homestead. The route was up a small twisting road into the foothills, then on a two-track into the coastal mountains and through a beautifully dense redwood stand. When we arrived at Kent's place we were far from anything and in the middle of a vast forest. I was immediately awestruck by the huge redwoods, isolation and splendor of nature around me. It was late and dark that deep in the woods so Kent explained I would see more in the morning. There was nothing but a small cabin where Kent lived. He parked the van next to the cabin and turned down the back seat to make into the bed.

Up to then, the evening had not been exceptional, but when I went into Kent's small cabin, it quickly became obvious why he was so secretive about his little bit of natural paradise - he was growing marijuana out there.

"So - you want a smoke?" asked Kent. He had pot plants all over the place in the cabin and was even drying some in his oven. Like most college kids in the late Sixties I had experimented with a couple of joints, but I was not a regular user and had never been high or enjoyed it. I wasn't opposed to pot smoking - I had plenty of friends who would be classified as weekend users. Like many things, I hadn't formed an opinion on marijuana use and was rather ambivalent to the whole thing.

Of course, I did not want to be rude after Kent had been so kind so I said, "Sure, what the Hell? It will be a good way to end the day."

"Its good stuff," said Kent. "You probably won't need much."

He was right. Very soon we were laughing about nothing and I was high. After about an hour of telling stories and laughing at each other, I went to my little trailer and slept very well.

The next morning the beauty of the surroundings engulfed me. The land was rich, moss covered and dominated by some of the biggest, grandest trees I had ever seen. But I also noticed the tree stumps all around. These stumps were the remains of the original trees of the area and were reminders of the logging that had gone on in this area. The stumps were huge - like everything else in the place. Many were ten to twelve feet high and eight to ten feet in diameter with a few much larger. It made me realize how big the original trees must have been.

The real surprise came later. After a cup of coffee, Kent showed me his current use for the stumps. He was growing pot on top of them. It was ingenious and the perfect spot. Not only could the plants not be seen from the ground, but the added height allowed the plants to get more sunlight and water than they would on the ground. And, as Kent added, "The cops can come through here and never see a thing." He had cut footsteps in the side of the stumps and would climb up every day to care for them, pick enough for sales and personal usage, then leave the rest alone.

Day two on the Pacific route had been a long, frustrating, but very memorable day. I had only gone about 150 miles and it had taken over twelve hours to cover that meager distance, but it was certainly one of the most impressionable parts of the trip up to Fort Lewis.

June 18

Well – it's now a little later & I am a soldier in Fort Lewis, Wash. (except I'm the only one who doesn't look like a soldier since my box hasn't arrived and I haven't any uniforms!) [More about that later.] Much has happened since my last writing and I probably won't have time to say it all around here. First impressions here are pretty good, but let me catch up first.

Back on the coast I finally got 2 rides up to Eureka, Cal. That means I covered about 100 miles in about 12 hours. At the time I felt really depressed & "bummed out", but I guess it really wasn't that bad! An interesting thing happened in Eureka. I was standing by the road looking for a ride through town. This guy came up and told me his boss was a writer and he just drove him all over the country. He wanted to know if I wanted to go to FLORIDA w/them! Sounded tempting, but Uncle Sam said No. But boy did I have a lot of things I could have told him. Sure would have liked to talk to that writer. I've got a best seller in my head!

Got picked up by Kent – said I could sleep at his "homestead". That's what it was. He was camping out in the hills east of Eureka on a friend's land – holding it for him so they could build a house there. Really was a nice guy. He let me sleep in the back end of his VW bus – best sleep in a while! [Kent] was really nice – even gave me breakfast! One thing about sleeping out in that forest was to see what the loggers have done to the N. Cal. forest. I was right in the middle of a second growth redwood forest. There were some HUGE stumps that used to be just fantastic gigantic trees. Those trees must have been so beautiful because the little ones were. When you see stumps about 8 – 12 ft. in diameter and about 8 – 10 ft. high, you have a hard time realizing how big the tree must have been. I did see some of the old redwoods in State and National parks, but I would love to see some more. Mr Reagan says "See one redwood, you've seen 'em all." But you couldn't be further from the truth Ronny – they are unbelievable and definitely a thing of God!

DRIVERS - DAY 2 NORTHBOUND

6. 2 mi. up Rt.1 - hermit looking guy

7. To Westport - guy & girl originally from Mich. - 2 other pick-ups - alone for once -

8. After long wait & long walk - to Leggit - strange guy in pick-up w/ 2 hitchhikers in front (including me) & 5 in back wild through the mts. told all about growing pot.

9. Up 101 to Eureka - guy & a BEAUTIFUL girl and a German shepherd - finally alone for a while - great couple.

10. Kent - through Eureka and let me stay at his homestead - just a cabin in the woods. Let me sleep in the back of his VW bus. fantastic guy (and his dog Muchka) Fed me, housed me, & then gave me a ride to Arcata next morning.

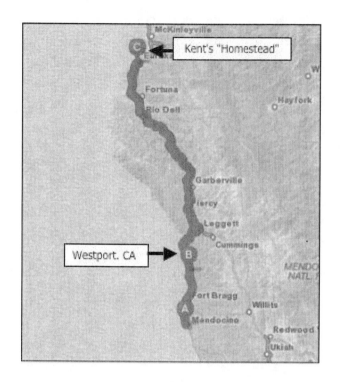

The Environment

As I wandered through the redwood forest around Kent's cabin, I started thinking about the beauty of nature and how humanity had mistreated it. The environment and environmental concerns became important to me during the summer of '71. I had not paid much attention to the various environmental activists I had heard on campus prior to the trip, but as I traveled west and saw some of the most spectacular scenery on earth, I started thinking about it more and more. By the time I got to Kent's homestead, it had become one of the dominant topics of the trip.

Today environmental considerations are a much more important and acceptable part of our social and economic world than in the early Seventies. At that time the environmental movement was just beginning, learning lessons from the Civil Rights Movement and the anti-war protesters about how to get their point across using peaceful protest and the media. Walking across campus at the University of Michigan in the late Sixties I heard speakers and saw protests against the environmental damage of the auto industry and concern about pollution in the Great Lakes. But these were usually small groups who appeared to be on the radical extreme. These were the "tree-huggers" and "greenies" that whined about environmental damage, but did not have many practical answers, especially considering the economic importance of industry to Michigan and the Midwest. We were not going to stop producing steel, plastics, or automobiles. That was the economic lifeblood of America. The industrialized America had won WWII and was fighting the dreaded communist threat of the Cold War. To suggest we somehow limit American industrial growth was tantamount to admitting you were a communist sympathizer, and we could not do that.

Throughout the trip, though, I continually saw the connection between the power of the Industrial/Agricultural complex and the waste and destruction they created. Outside Gary, Indiana, the smokestacks and smog of the U.S. Steel plants and other related industry demonstrated both the successes and failures of American industry. Had industrial might made the United States the leading political and economic power in the world? Definitely. Had it provided millions of jobs and comfortable middle class lives for American workers? Of course. Had it made the 1950's and 1960's some of the most prosperous times in our history? Arguably yes. But, in the process, it had destroyed natural habitats, brought many animals to the point of extinction, and created economic disparity we still have not overcome. The massive industrialized farms seen on the Great Plains also contributed to this problem, since they used and abused the environment as much as the manufacturing segment of society.

I noticed these things and thought about it while heading west through the plains and the Rocky Mountains, but it really hit me when thumbing up the coastal highways of California. Aunt Becky had a lot to do with my newly discovered thoughts regarding environmentalism. Aunt Becky – and all the Green family for that matter – always had a wonderfully idyllic, slightly naive, vision of the earth and the beauty of the land. Aunt Becky's life in the north San Francisco Bay area surrounded by Mt. Tamalpais, the redwoods, and the ocean, undoubtedly made her a quiet, but thoughtful, supporter of environmental protection. My excursions to Muir Redwoods and Yosemite put a stamp on my mind about the need to protect our environment.

Traveling through northern California I saw massive swaths of mountainsides clear-cut and exposed by lumbering companies. The night spent with my pot-growing friend in the redwood forest further emphasized the need to conserve those gentle giants. My comments in the journal are a bit short and innocent, but the memory of those massive stumps and the image of the original growth forest stuck with me. A realization came that there had to be a way to balance nature's needs and industry's needs. There had to be a way to successfully maintain our industrial and agricultural might and still conserve our natural beauty and environment.

Environmental issues are a much larger concern today, but we still need to increase our understanding and work to achieve a balance. The environmental movement has become more mainstream and is now an accepted part of our social/political landscape. All levels of government have offices responsible for studying environmental impact, businesses now look for ways to conserve natural resources, and society expects environmental issues to be part of the discussion for new developments. Green technology and products are becoming more affordable and profitable. People readily acknowledge the need to protect our environment and conserve. Being green is considered cool. This is a credit to those radicals and protesters back in the Sixties who would not be dissuaded from their message by industrial money or threats, and also to the environmental scientists and researchers who were underfunded and harassed in their investigations. It is another example of how far we have come in the last forty years.

But money still talks. When jobs are threatened, environmental regulations are ignored or modified to allow job creation. When the nation becomes concerned about importing oil, we start talking about drilling on the protected North Slope of Alaska or more deep water drilling in the Gulf of Mexico - even though we have learned the hard way how a minor leak can cause devastating damage to the ecosystem. When the coal, oil, or gas industries need more customers, the Environmental Protection Agency is blamed for intrusive regulation. Laws such as the Clean Air Act are relaxed to give big industries more liberty to produce energy at the expense of the environment. This is where the balance must take place. We must realize we cannot produce products, or create jobs, or extract natural resources without consideration to the future damage to the earth. Unfortunately, environmental concerns are going to remain secondary until financial gains are seen in saving and conserving the earth. When money can be made by conserving energy, saving forests, or keeping pollutants out of waterways, then, and only then, will environmental concerns be on equal footing with manufacturing and business.

Traveling through Northern California gave me plenty of time to think about environmental issues. I had not taken many science classes in college and did not know a lot of statistics about the environment, but that did not stop me from looking for some sort of solution. What I did understand was the history of industrialization and how it had affected the environment and society in the past.

At the end of the 19th century and the beginning of the 20th century American industrial giants like Carnegie, Rockefeller, Ford, Gary, and others did not worry about the environmental impact when building their industrial empires. They were much more intent on building success and wealth. Today the same situation is occurring in China, India, Brazil, and other developing nations. They understand how the destruction of the rain forest, the burning of soft coal, the pollution of rivers, or the draining of aquifers are causing irreparable environmental change. But thousands of jobs are being created and economic prosperity is being introduced to poor nations. For example, a vast amount of fertile land is being opened for farming by clear cutting the rain forest in the Amazon Basin. This is damaging the land and endangering numerous animal species, but it is also creating jobs and huge profits for individuals and the Brazilian government. It is no different than when lumber barons bought the ancient hardwood forest of Michigan and clear-cut the northern Lower Peninsula in the 1870's. It was justified by the wealth and prominence it brought the area and in particular to a few rich and politically powerful men. The environmental damage was overshadowed by the economic impact of the operation. To be concerned about environmental damage implies you are concerned about the future. Why be concerned about the future when you can have the wealth of the world today? That is not a recent phenomenon. That philosophy is as old as history. Throughout history, humans have made and shaped the earth to their immediate needs, regardless of the consequences for the future.

The Industrial Revolution of Great Britain in the late 18th and early 19th century is recognized as one of the great turning points in history. It affected the entire spectrum of British and European life. Similarly, industrial growth in China is quickly making China an economic, industrial and political power in the 21st century. Like 19th century England, the Chinese have very little consideration for the smog, pollution, or toxic waste they are producing. China is damming rivers, burning soft coal, and making as much power as they can as fast as they can. Their cities are growing faster than they can build as workers come in from the provinces only to find very low pay, slums, and extreme poverty. The same can be said for India. Neither of these nations is very concerned about the environment. That would get in the way of their growth. A positive of all this is that their workers are making more money, their citizens are demanding and expecting more voice in the government, and their governments are becoming more visible and involved in worldwide political / economic matters than ever before.

All these changes in the third world nations are no different than the United States at the end of the 19th century as we began our industrial revolution. Open immigration provided us with a wonderful source of cheap labor. Seemingly unlimited supplies of natural resources gave us the power we needed. The government was easily influenced to look the other way to help industrial growth and gain economic power. But, of course, all this success led to overcrowded cities, slums, toxic waste, a huge financial disparity between rich and poor, and numerous other problems associated with our industrial growth. If we made money, provided jobs and helped the American government become strong, then it was all worthwhile. That was good capitalist philosophy. That was the American way. There were many problems created that are now starting to be corrected. But there is more to be done. There must to be a balance between the environmental concerns and successful industrial / agricultural growth. We need to continue to push forward and overcome the obstacles, keeping in mind what is good for the future is also good for today.

When I looked around Northern California in 1971 I saw a place of tranquil beauty and solitude. It was also an area of a very profitable logging industry. The beauty of the wilderness and the demands of the lumbermen created an early test of America's environmentalists to preserve the land and also provide jobs and economic gain for the area. Their successes and failures helped spread the national awareness of environmental con- servation. Those early attempts to limit encroachment on the redwoods and wilderness of California in the Sixties and Seventies can be used as a model of other nations around the world today. Hopefully we can find the needed balance between environmental concerns and economic demands in today's world too.

Sometimes a Good Drink Helps

After spending an hour admiring the redwoods around Kent's cabin, we went back into town and he dropped me off on the road north of Eureka. This was the start of another crazy day in northern California. Along with two other hitchhikers, I was picked up just north of Eureka and outside Arcata by two young men. I had planned on continuing up the coast, but when the driver, who looked to be about twenty years old, decided to head east toward Redding, I said, "What the Hell. It will get me to Interstate 5 quicker."

Shortly after we started the passenger said to me, "Hey, reach under your seat. There should be a bottle there."

I reached below the seat and behold, there was a full bottle of whiskey. "Hey, look what I found!" I exclaimed.

"Well, take a hit and pass it around."

"Damn! This is rotten stuff," I said after downing a full swallow. "But it does feel good going down."

"Well, don't drink it all - pass it here."

So, the four of us - the driver wisely passed on the party - proceeded to pass the bottle. Since the booze was warm, and we were all trying to prove our macho pride by drinking it straight, it did not take too long before we had finished it and were drunk. I think I faded into a gentle nap for a few minutes, but was awakened when the car pulled to a stop at the side of the road. When my eyes focused I saw we were parked at a deserted spot next to what was ironically named Whiskeytown Lake just west of Redding.

"Wha's happenin'?" I drunkenly asked.

"We're goin' swimmin'! Come on, let's go!"

"What the heck - You guys just going skinny-dipping right out here at the roadside?"

"Yeah, sure! Nobody's going to see us. Come on. You chicken?"

Of course, after challenging my courage, I couldn't say no. I quickly stripped off my clothes and jumped in.

"Jeeeesus Christ! This water's freezing!" I said once I caught my breath.

"Yep - wakes you up doesn't it".

It was the middle of a very hot afternoon and we were only about fifty yards from a busy road, but we were all drunk and uninhibited enough that we were not worried about much of anything. The water was extremely cold and sobered us up. We splashed around for twenty or thirty minutes before we continued on our way. Looking back now there was a tremendous quotient of danger in this little escapade but at the time we did not think about getting arrested for indecent exposure, public drunkenness, or even a swimming accident. Those are the things you look back on with maturity and say how stupid it was – but at the time was a great adventure.

Shortly after swimming, my bar-tending driver turned south on Interstate 5. He dropped me off on an entrance ramp already loaded with other hitchhikers looking for rides north. I took my appropriate spot at the end of the line and waited for a ride. But it was very hot - about 95 degrees - and my head was killing me. By now the whiskey buzz was wearing off. As I stood in the heat I became dehydrated, had a splitting headache, and a terrible case of cotton-mouth. I felt like shit and did not really care if I got another ride. I had not eaten all day - only drank whiskey - and needed some food, water, and air conditioning, so I walked across the street to the nearby Denny's Restaurant. I was exhausted and plopped in the first open booth. After two glasses of water and a cheap hamburger I felt a little better. I felt even better when the girl in the neighboring booth leaned over and said, "I saw your bags when you came in. Where you headed? I'm going to Eugene if that would help."

Well, of course going to Eugene, Oregon would help, and anyway, how could I turn down a ride with a young co-ed? Nancy was not beautiful - she was a little short and pudgy - but she had an attractive face, a pleasant smile, and was very intelligent. So I climbed into her Volkswagen Beetle and proceeded to make small talk and dreamed of getting lucky that night. Given all the crazy things that had happened in the last 48 hours - getting stranded in Westport, picked up by a joint-smoking, dog loving couple, spending the night at a pot farm, and drinking my way across northern California - it seemed appropriate I should get picked up by a young woman open to a little hanky-panky.

If I had been realistic, I would have known nothing was going to happen. Most of my female friends always said I was a good listener and a nice guy, but I wasn't especially romantic or a smooth-talking hustler. I was not a hunk or the irresistible type, so it was natural Nancy found me non-threatening and easy to talk to. We talked, laughed, and had a nice ride north to Eugene.

Things sure have changed since 1971. Today there are very few young college females who would randomly pick up a stranger in a Denny's Restaurant and take them almost 200 miles up the road without considering their safety. But in the early Seventies it was not unusual. Even girls could hitchhike alone without any great fear or reservations. While I'm sure there were cases of muggings, rape, and theft from violent hitch-hikers, there was very little media attention to that sort of thing and you did not hear of it happening with any great frequency.

Being a hormone charged twenty-one year old, there were plenty of fantasies throughout the summer journey of having a rollicking one-night stand with some beautiful woman. There were a number of young women I met during the summer, and each of them proved to be just as helpful, sweet and innocent as Nancy. And being as I was just as innocent in my own way, nothing ever came of my fantasies. A guy can always dream though. We did not get to Eugene until 2:30 a.m., and by then I knew my dreams of sex were not going to happen. School was not in session and the dorms were closed to visitors, so I ended up spending the night in the back of Nancy's Beetle, which meant I slept very little. However, I had traveled over 450 miles that day, and I was much closer to Fort Lewis.

Journal from June 18 continued:

Got picked up outside Arcata, Cal. by a guy going to Lakeview, Ore. I thought it was on the route I wanted to go on, up the coast some more and through more red-wood forests. Instead he turned and went straight across the state towards Redding! So I missed the last bit of coast and some other things I wanted to see. I was rather depressed because of missing that & because I was taking a longer way around. I was kinda getting down in the dumps when the passenger (there was a driver, passenger, & 2 other hitchhikers) pulled out a fifth of whiskey. The driver didn't drink, but the rest of us sure did!

The ride went rather quickly after that, but I sure paid for it when I got dropped off in Redding. It was very warm there and the sun & the booze did not mix too well. Needless to say I didn't feel real great there. After I got dropped off on a ramp w/ 11 other h-hikers I got fed up & went over to a restaurant for dinner. When I came in w/all my stuff, this girl next to me leaned over and asked how far I was going! Well – she said she'd take me to Eugene – which was on my route! Well, I guess it must be every male hitchhikers dream to get picked up by a beautiful, horny, nymphomaniac female who will ask him discreetly if he needs a place to stay that night. And of course that NEVER happens. But naturally, since I am a"normal" male, etc. I had these same, nasty, unpuritanical, filthy thoughts. (Ah heck – gimme a break!) And, of course, Nancy was one of the nicest – that's NICEST – girls that ever came off the Mayflower! But she was fun to talk to and really a good kid. We got into Eugene & the U. of Ore. about 2:30 A.M. All the way she had promised I could sleep w/ some friends of hers – so I was planning on a nice sleep. Unfortunately, since school had just gone home the dorms were not allowing visitors for fear of theft. Sooooo – I slept in the back end of her VW bug, which is rather small and uncomfortable to say the least. But I guess it was a bed! So I got about 5 hrs. sleep at the most!

DRIVERS - DAY 3 NORTHBOUND

11. Arcata - Redding: 2 guys going to Lakeview, Ore. When I first got in I thought they were heading my way up the coast -they didn't - went straight across the state! Had 2 other h-hikers. all except the driver split a 5th of whiskey - whew! Swam in reservoir.

12. Ride through town to ramp w/ other hikers (10 already on the ramp)

13. To Eugene, Ore. w/Nancy - met her in restaurant- got in about 2:30 AM - slept in back of her VW. Ouch

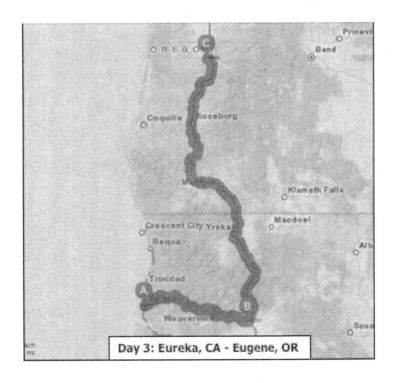

Day 3: Eureka, CA - Eugene, OR

The Colonel

Early the next morning Nancy drove me back to the highway. She was sweet, considerate, and I was very appreciative of her help. Shortly after getting to the highway, I got a ride north to Portland, Oregon.

In Portland I found myself on the wrong end of a long line of hitchhikers on the south side of the bridge over the Columbia River. Word had spread through the grapevine that hitchhikers were not welcome in the state of Washington and were frequently harassed and arrested. Consequently, everyone wanted to get a ride in Oregon to take them far into Washington. There were twelve to fifteen other thumbers in front of me when I got to the bridge and the prospects of getting a ride were dim.

As I stood there I noticed most of the hitchhikers were long-haired and looked like they had been on the road for days. Many had signs saying "Seattle," "Vancouver," or "Canada" - the latter two destinations implying they were heading north to avoid the draft. It was going to be a long wait.

Then I noticed a driver who went past all the long-hairs and stopped to pick up a soldier in uniform. As I watched this a brilliant thought popped into my head. I could use the military connection to my advantage. My hair was still short – not military length yet, but I had always had short hair and had not changed it during the trip – so I decided to be more specific with my destination. I pulled out a pen and made a sign that read "Fort Lewis". Within minutes an old pickup truck stopped. The driver was a very straight laced looking gentleman with his teenage son as a passenger. He had passed by all the others before stopping for me. This, of course, was breaking one of the unwritten rules of the road by jumping ahead of my fellow hitchers, but another rule of the road was that it was fair to do whatever possible to get a ride.

"Heading to Fort Lewis, eh? You must be going to Boot Camp."

"Well, yes Sir," I replied with good military formality. My driver looked to be in his early fifties, was trim, fit, with a butch cut and a very serious expression on his face. His whole manner told me a little formality was the right thing to do. "I'm due there for ROTC training."

"Glad to help you out then," he said. "All the other hitchhikers back there were long-haired hippies. I was going to keep right on going, but I saw your sign for Fort Lewis and figured you must be doing some sort of military service. I'm not going to give any of those God-damned hippies a ride, but I'm happy to help out a young man who is willing to do his patriotic duty. I'm a retired army lieutenant colonel. Went to 'Nam in 1965. Spent a year as a battalion operations officer. It was tough, but I did my part. I just can't stand those whinny-ass commie lovers."

"Well thank you Sir, I really appreciate the ride." I decided it would be best if I just agreed with him. When asked, I gave him a quick explanation of what I expected at ROTC Summer Camp and a quick summary of the events of my trip. But I felt he wanted to use me to express his own feelings about the war in Vietnam.

"You're a great example for my son here. I'm sure proud there are still young men like you willing to join the military and do your duty to your country. It seems all we hear about now days are the war protesters and the draft dodgers," he said. "We've got to stand strong against those communists. We can't let them take over Southeast Asia! Do you know how weak that would make the U.S. look? I can't stand the thought of it!"

He continued talking without really waiting for my response. "If we don't stop 'em there, the next thing we know they will be taking over Portland or Seattle. Their goal is world domination you know! I'm really proud of you - that you're willing to stand up to them!"

"Well thank you Sir," was about all I could say. The problem was, I really did not know how I felt, and I wasn't too keen on the idea of "standing up to the commies". I did understand and sympathize with many of the ideas of the anti-war movement. I had many friends - including a couple roommates at school - who were very opposed to the war and the draft. But I just agreed with him and thought about what the colonel had to say because he seemed to be speaking for a large segment of the American population.

The colonel was a vivid reminder of the gap that had developed in America over the Vietnam War and the generational differences that existed. Most of my previous rides had been with other youth, or at least people who did not talk much politics. But this particular driver made it clear he did not care at all for any of those "peace-niks" and "long-hairs." He proceeded to castigate the hippies, the peace movement, and anyone who could possibly be critical of our efforts to stop the spread of communism in the world, "Because I'd rather we fight them over there than here on the shores of America!"

My driver assumed I agreed with him, otherwise there would not be any rational reason I would be going to Fort Lewis and ROTC training camp. I quietly sat and agreed with him, not knowing which of his arguments I agreed with and which I disagreed with. What became obvious though was I had not had a driver with such strong opinions on the war in quite a few days. It reinforced something I already knew, but needed a little reminder of – there were two sides to every political argument and both sides usually only listened to the information that best fit their opinion. Prior to the colonel picking me up most of my drivers had been young, more liberal people who hid pot in their back-yards, hid whiskey under their seats, or were college students opposed to the war. Now I was hearing arguments from a man who had been in the military and a more conservative view.

This last day was only about 275 miles and, because of my luck in Portland, only took me about six hours. I got to Seattle in plenty of time to look around and get established.

Journal of June 18 continued:

Got a ride to Portland from there. Wanted to make sure I got a ride through Wash. Because they are suppose to be real TOUGH on h-hikers there. Of course it was illegal in Wyoming, Utah & Nevada, but nobody cared too much there. So I stood on the x-way w/more hikers w/my little sign for Seattle. After standing around for a while w/no luck I began thinking about the GI in uniform I saw get picked up in about 2 sec. by an elderly couple while 10 "long-hairs" stood there gapping. Sooo, while I waited I turned my sign over and printed "Ft. Lewis" on it. And guess what – about 5 minutes later a pick-up w/a man and his son in it stopped. He had just retired from the army (30 year ROTC man who had just retired as a Lt. Colonel) and picked me up because of my "Ft Lewis" sign. So we talked army and school, etc. all the way up to the fort. From there I got a ride right away w/a GI going to downtown Seattle.

DRIVERS - DAY 4 NORTHBOUND

14. to Portland w/guy & 4 other hikers. One was a Jesus freak - interesting.

15 & 16. 2 rides through Portland

17. w/sign for Ft. Lewis ride w/Lt. Col. (retired) & his son to Tacoma - interesting Army talk.

18. Soldier to downtown Seattle

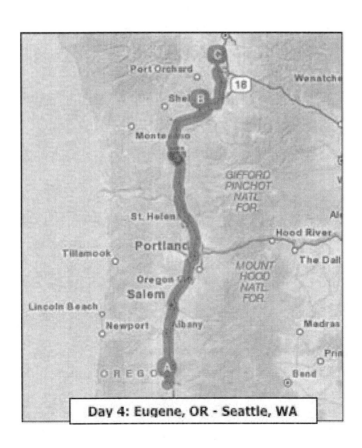

Day 4: Eugene, OR - Seattle, WA

The Cold War & Vietnam

Listening to the colonel made me think about the Vietnam War for the first time in many days. Aunt Becky and I had discussed it a little, but not too seriously and without any strong opinions either for or against. Otherwise, the subject had not come up since my ride with Joe the trucker on the first day of my trip. Being part of the Baby Boomer Generation – those born between 1945 and 1960 – my life had been influenced strongly by the Cold War and the Vietnam War. As I got closer to Fort Lewis and my military training, I realized America's policies toward communism were going to impact my future and it was time for me to start making some decisions about how I felt.

The Cold War – the political, economic, and philosophical competition between the United States and the Union of Soviet Socialist Republics – impacted just about everything that happened in American life from the end of World War II, in 1945, until the collapse of the U.S.S.R. in 1991. Historical events such as the Korean War, the Cuban Missile Crisis, the Berlin Wall, and of course the Vietnam War resulted from the Cold War. The arms race, the space program, songs, clothing, movies, advertising, and much more were all affected by our up and down relationship with the communist world.

In the 21st century our enemies are terrorists. They do not even have to be associated with any particular nation or group – the reference to terrorism is enough to send our society into a frenzy. No event in the twenty-first century has influenced America as much as the terrorist attacks of September 11, 2001. Since then we have been inundated with concerns over terrorism. Today the threat of terrorism can cause political and economic systems to go into a tail-spin. Culturally we have movies, television, and games devoted to unnamed terrorists and their threat. Just the word terrorist denotes hatred and fear.

For the latter half of the twentieth century the term "communist" had the same connotation. There was no bigger insult during the Fifties and Sixties than to be called a "commie". Opposition to the anti-communist, capitalistic ideals of the U.S. government was seen as unpatriotic and treasonous by many. Most Americans were fearful of the possibility of nuclear war with the Soviet Union. Europe was divided into communist and free and the Iron Curtain was never going to come down in our lifetime.

Cartoons like *Rocky and Bullwinkle* had bad guys with Russian accents. In the movies – like a James Bond movie - the enemy was communist. In books, magazines, music, and even fashion took an East vs.

West theme. Even sporting events became political, as any games between the U.S. and the U.S.S.R. took on extra significance.

When I was teaching the history of the Cold War to students in the 21st century, many of the events seemed almost comical - exemplified by the notion that hiding under an elementary school desk would save children from nuclear annihilation. Watching propaganda films of the dangers of communist infiltration and conquest of the world can make today's students laugh. But at the time they were very serious. Looking back on those times it is obvious much of the Cold War was a lot of bluff, propaganda, and political face-saving moves on both sides. But there was a threat, and it had to be taken seriously.

The Cold War directly affected my family. In 1966, both my brothers were involved in the Vietnam War. Fred was fighting, and being wounded by, communists in the jungles and Gary was on a destroyer patrolling the coast of Vietnam. From 1973 to 1976 I was stationed in Germany protecting our NATO allies and training to stop the communists if they attacked West Germany from East Germany. Was the communist threat real to my family while we were serving our nation? Yes, without a doubt. If you had told any of us communism in Eastern Europe would collapse, the Berlin Wall would come down without a fight, or the Soviet Union would be peacefully broken up and Russia would become an ally of the United States on many issues - if you had told anyone in the late Sixties or early Seventies those historical events would come to pass peacefully - we would have laughed in your face. We knew those things would never happen.

The Vietnam War was the most significant event of the Cold War. The United States became involved in Southeast Asia when France lost control in 1954. The U.S. government was committed to containing the spread of communism and helping democracies take hold around the world. We were convinced in the "domino theory" - that if one small nation became communist, all of the neighboring countries would fall to communism like a set of dominos. Today it seems naive and simplistic, but at the time it was an accepted policy and given credence by the communists who spoke of spreading their system around the world.

By 1964 the idea of stopping communism in Southeast Asia had become an important part of our foreign policy. President Johnson stated he was "Not going to be the President who saw Southeast Asia go the way China went." and when the *U.S.S. Maddox* was fired upon in the Gulf of Tonkin, Johnson had all the justification he needed to increase our presence in the area.

While the Gulf of Tonkin Incident is now considered an example of political power play and propaganda, at the time it was a valid justification for war. Almost 100% of Congress and 75% of all Americans supported Johnson's call to increase American involvement in Vietnam and stop the spread of communism in the region. Unfortunately, that involvement continued to escalate and America found itself stuck in a position difficult to get out of without loss of prestige and power.

The sad thing is, America did not learn from its own history. President George W. Bush's invasion of Iraq in 2003 had amazing similarities to Vietnam - from Congress's overwhelming approval of the invasion, evidence of trumped up causes, a long drawn out war against seemingly inferior military forces, and the public's steadily increasing disapproval of the conflict.

Every generation has something that shapes its mentality and direction. For today's generation it was the events of 9/11. For my parents, those events were the Great Depression and World War II. For my brothers Gary and Fred, the prosperity and stability of the Fifties and early Sixties impacted their lives. For my generation the historical event was the Vietnam War. For young Americans growing up in the late Sixties and early Seventies, the Vietnam War not only affected politics, but also the economy, society, and culture. For my generation it defined who we were and what we did in our lives more than anything else. In many ways, it still does.

Some historical events have united our nation - World War II, the landing on the moon, or the recent terrorist attacks on America for instance - but the Vietnam War created some of the most extreme divisions of attitudes and political ideology of the twentieth century. Many supported the anti-communist policies of the government. Generally people supported the war because of a fear of communism and what it represented to our way of life in the United States. Many believed defeat in Vietnam would result in the collapse of United States prestige and would be a major blow in our ongoing ideological conflict with the Soviet Union. Patriotic demonstrations and marches were designed to show support for the war, the military, and the government.

But in the late Sixties and early Seventies a growing number of Americans became disillusioned by our involvement in Southeast Asia. As the war dragged on, more and more joined the anti-war movement, especially the nation's youth. The war was fought primarily by young draftees with an average age of only nineteen. As casualties mounted, the anti-war movement grew.

Learning from the Civil Rights Movement, anti-war demonstrators learned how to use the media to spread their message. Demonstrations were scheduled to coincide with media coverage. By taking advantage of television coverage the anti-war message got more people involved wand slowly made an impact on the American public. As more protests made the news and more bad news came from overseas, more citizens thought about the war and what it was about. In the end, the media had a dramatic effect on attitudes toward the war.

By the summer of '71 anti-war protests were quite common on campus. The University of Michigan had a national reputation for its anti-war movement. Ameri-

ca's involvement in Vietnam was a topic at every venue
on campus and there were many late night debates
about the pros and cons of our involvement among my
roommates and friends. As a result, my own thinking
about the war and the military became confused and
conflicted. I had been raised to be patriotic and support the nation. I had brothers who had served in
Vietnam. I had friends who had been drafted and
killed. But I also had friends who were adamant in
their disapproval of the war. I was personally exposed
to the anti-war protests on campus. Just a year before
my journey, in May 1970, campuses across the nation -
including the University of Michigan - exploded in
protests over President Nixon's decision to bomb Cam-
bodia. This, or course, resulted in the famous shooting
of four students at Kent State University. Those kill-
ings took a personal turn. I remember my mother
watching the news of Kent State and saying, "My God, if
they are going to start killing our own children, it's time
to get out of there."

As the war dragged on, many Americans started
questioning the conduct of the war, our goals in the
area, and if it was worth the price. Almost every night,
as we sat around the dinner table, the evening news
would have the latest from Vietnam, body counts, and
pictures of the wounded being evacuated. These were
not the censured war photos from WWII or Korea.
These were pictures of young Americans being killed
and wounded broadcast into people's living room. This
was war as most had never seen it. As more and more
young people protested the war, the justifications for

fighting became weaker and weaker and the so called "light at the end of the tunnel" became dimmer and dimmer.

The war greatly impacted politics. The political decisions of Presidents Kennedy, Johnson, Nixon, and Ford, and the decisions of their Congresses were all influenced by events in Vietnam. It also increased partisan political debate. The Democratic Party became split between anti-war democrats and more moderate Johnson/Humphrey Democrats who supported the war effort. The Republican Party was able to take advantage of that weakness and win the next elections.

The economic affects were more subtle. Our nation's debt grew as we borrowed to finance the war. The military-industrial complex grew at a rapid rate and made huge profits building war materials. Federal money for social programs – like President Johnson's "Great Society" to help the poor – was diverted to pay for the war. And of course, the war determined who we traded with, what we bought, who we sold to, and where our money was spent.

Vietnam dominated every discussion in one way or another. Every neighborhood gathering, business meeting, or social event could become a debate about the military, the draft, or events in Southeast Asia. Soon after graduating and entering the army, I was visiting a friend who had an informal get-together. I was casually meeting people when a conversation occurred that illustrated the divisiveness of the war. I introduced myself to a neighbor and she asked me what I did for a living.

"I'm a second lieutenant in the army," I proudly replied.

"Oh, a baby-killer! That's too bad." And she turned and walked away without any further discussion. I was so flabbergasted by her response I did not know what to say. Even though I had not been to Vietnam and had only been in the military for a couple of months, she had formed her opinion and was not willing to talk about anything, even neighborly small talk, with someone who represented the other side.

Historically, all youthful generations have a period of rebelliousness and wanting to be different - but The Vietnam War and the draft made my generation more active and involved than previous generations. The music, movies, and fashion of the Sixties all reflected the war's impact on our society, but nothing impacted the young men of the late Sixties as much as the draft. We were the first generation to be significantly impacted by the draft.

The draft had been around since World War I, and men were drafted in World War II, Korea, and during the Fifties, but until the Vietnam War occurred the draft was not too controversial. Previous wars had many volunteers and enlistments, so the draft was more supplementary, but that changed in the late Sixties. With the expanding military involvement in

Southeast Asia, and increasing death rates after 1965, the draft became an institution affecting every young male.

Upon turning eighteen every male had to register for the draft. If he did not want to go into the military a young man had to consider how the draft would affect his future. The odds were if he did not do anything he would receive his draft notice, so he had to think about his options. Would he go to college? If so, that only delayed the question. Would he get a job right out of high school? That could be interrupted by being drafted. Should he get married? Should he enlist? Should he try to avoid the draft by fleeing to Canada, never to return to the U.S? Or should he take his chances on the draft lottery and hope for a high number which would mean he would be exempt?

In addition to those basic questions was the added complication of the racial and economic prejudice that became an unintentional consequence of the draft. African Americans and poor whites did not have as many options available to avoid the draft and made up a much larger percentage of the draftees than well-to-do whites. The social inequality of the system provided another argument for anti-war protesters. All these things had to be considered before most young men had even graduated from high school.

These decisions, of course, did not just affect the individual, but also the family and friends of young Americans. By the time I graduated from high school in

1968, many of my classmates had already enlisted and were serving in Vietnam. Two had been seriously wounded and one killed - before their classmates had even graduated from high school. That was typical of high schools throughout the United States.

Consequently, Vietnam forced a young man to make important decisions early in his life. It was complicated and had long term implications. Looking back it seems relatively simple - you were either for the war and willing to go to 'Nam, or you were against the war and would oppose it. But it was not that cut and dried.

The political divisions and generational differences of the Vietnam War grew as we became more and more involved. While the media's coverage influenced people's opinions about the war, it was nothing compared to the cover of today. In 1971 news and information came via the six o'clock news on one of three national media outlets that generally said the same thing. Otherwise, you had to read the newspapers and magazines and do some research on your own to shape your opinions and ideas. Today the visual and electronic media has grown with the advent of twenty-four hour news, digital technology, and social networking. It is hard not to be inundated with information. In many ways it is more difficult to develop your own political, social ideas today. Modern media does so much to influence lifestyle and access to information that it is difficult to get unbiased, factual information without some political slant to it.

One of the major problems with getting out of Vietnam was the perception that America had never lost a war. Americans could not fathom the idea of losing a war and just giving up on our commitment to the South Vietnamese before all our goals had been accomplished. Unfortunately, our goals were unclear, vague, and obscure to most people, so we did not know what we were trying to accomplish. We said we wanted to stop the spread of communism, but that did not seem possible, or even necessary the longer we were in Vietnam. We were supposedly defending the democratic government of South Vietnam, but that government became autocratic, oppressive, and uncooperative with the U.S. As a result, most of the goals, and reasons, for being there became moot.

A significant lesson learned - once we did get out of Vietnam - was that America's prestige, economy, and worldwide influence did not suffer. After getting out of Southeast Asia our dealings with the Soviet Union improved with the passage of nuclear test ban treaties and better trade leading up to the Soviet collapse in 1991. Today, Vietnam is a prosperous nation and a frequent vacation spot for American tourists. This is a lesson our nation needs to remember when debating the pros and cons of our current involvement in the Middle East and Afghanistan.

With historical hindsight, the Vietnam War seems unnecessary, because the conflict did nothing to bring about the end of communism. When the Berlin Wall fell in 1989 and Eastern Europe became free, many

Americans kept waiting for the Soviets to send in tanks and militarily reassert themselves. It did not happen. When the Soviet Union collapsed in 1991 it seemed even more remarkable to a generation that had lived in fear of a Soviet nuclear attack. The interesting thing about the fall of the Iron Curtain and the U.S.S.R. was it was done peacefully with very little loss of life and virtually no military involvement by the United States. American historians like to point to the pressure and increased military spending of the Reagan administration and how it led to the bankruptcy of the Soviet economy, but I believe the collapse of communism was a result of improved trade and communications around the world. I have always believed Eastern Europe's communist societies collapsed because of "McDonald's, blue jeans, and rock and roll." The people of Eastern Europe saw the economic prosperity and social freedoms of the West and demanded those benefits in their homelands. When the communist system could not provide it, the people demanded, and finally produced a change.

In 1971 I still hadn't formed a strong opinion about Vietnam. I was a proud American and believed in our way of life and had been brought up to have respect for the decisions made by our government. I did not want to allow the spread of communism, nor did I like the idea of pulling out and admitting defeat. A large part of me believed we were over there for a good cause and a justifiable reason. But I also believed the war and the draft were unfair. I wasn't sure it would hurt American prestige if we honestly admitted our mistakes and got out. I felt the American people were not being told the whole story by our government. It also bothered me that America's image was being badly tarnished throughout the rest of the world. Having a four year commitment of military service, which in all likelihood meant I would have to go to Vietnam, only complicated matters. I needed to justify the war to myself so I could do my duty with pride and commitment. At the same time, I was hoping against hope I would not have to go. The Vietnam War became a personal conflict that affected me and my future.

Thus, the Colonel, as my last driver before I put on army fatigues, seemed a fitting balance to the political and social divisions dividing the United States in 1971. Soon I would have to make up my own mind on how I fit into all that mess.

Steve McQueen Was Right

The book, <u>On The Loose</u>, had a quote by the actor Steve McQueen saying, "I would rather wake up in the middle of nowhere than on any city on Earth." I understood McQueen better after I visited Seattle. I enjoyed Seattle, but the entire day of sight-seeing I felt lonely, even though I was with two fellow hitchhikers I had met on the road. I missed the openness, freedom, and independence of the road. I missed the self-paced, easy schedule, and felt crowded and claustrophobic. This feeling would come again later in the summer when visiting London and Paris. I had hitchhiked over 3600 miles and rarely felt alone. I had enjoyed time to reflect on life while hitchhiking and waiting for rides, but in the city I felt I had to be going somewhere and doing something. Seattle was a good place to unwind and have free time before going to camp. It was easy going, relaxed, and provided a good transition from the road to the organization of military life. Things would change in a hurry once I got to Fort Lewis.

Steve McQueen Was Right

Journal of June 18 continued:

So I made it to the big city of the Northwest. Walked around and looked at the city (it was Weds. afternoon) [June 16]. It really is a beautiful city! Very nice. That night, as I was riding a bus out to a park to sleep I met 2 other h-hikers I had met on the road. As we talked about our adventures a guy leaned over and joined the conversation. He then invited us all to the use of his floor for the night. The next day we all went for a tour of the town. It sure is great to have someone else to walk around with. The loneliest places in the world are the places where there are the most people. I haven't felt lonely at all on the road – even my 4 hr. stand on the coast. I was probably closer to people and things than ever before. And definitely a lot more sensitive to feelings, friendliness, and other people. But the coldness & crowd of the big city can get to you. Everyone has a place to go, someone to see, and something to do – except you! The peace and quiet of Mother Nature can be much friendlier than any city man has yet built and so many of the people in them. So I was glad to have someone to walk with. You don't notice the crowds and you feel so much more like you're in the crowd w/friends around. So we walked around town and had a good time, eating fish on the wharf, drinking beer in the park w/the winos and goofing off. That night I got a room in the Mayflower Hotel right downtown and got a nice room and bath and plenty of rest for my last night. Felt good.

The Summer of '71

Friday, June 18: Got my military haircut, then hit the bus station.

The Northwest is an interesting region. It isn't as hilly or mountainous around here as I figured. We are in a big valley that is really quite flat, but the mts. are all around. The Olympic Mts. are visible to the west & the Cascades to the east – w/ Mt. Rainer dominating the entire scene. That old volcano is really something. It just keeps going up and can be seen from anywhere – if it's not raining. An old Indian tale here goes "If you can't see Mt Rainer it's raining – and if you can see it – it's going to rain." Seems like a pretty good way of predicting the weather here. We've had lots of rain so far. But it's also easy to see why the Indians worshipped the mt as a God! It is so amazing and powerful looking.

Becoming a Soldier

"Welcome to Fort Lewis cadet," said the sergeant. "Please take your orientation packet and follow the white line to station number one."

That was it, I was in the army. As I obediently followed the white line I found myself with a quiet group of male college students looking around inquisitively at the surroundings. I was part of Company C of the 2nd Training Battalion and was bussed off, with about twenty other current arrivals, to our barracks. Thus began my basic training at Fort Lewis.

By 1968, when I graduated from high school, I had been thinking about the Vietnam War and military service for some time. From my family background most people thought I would be "gung-ho" about the military, with Gary and Fred going to Annapolis and West Point respectively and still actively serving. But our family was on the fence about America's involvement in Southeast Asia. My father saw our activity in Vietnam as a necessary evil – he did not like it, but he was part of the generation who did not question the government's policies. Mother was more skeptical and was more opposed to the war the longer we were there. My own feelings were also mixed. Simply put, I did not have a definitive opinion.

I applied to West Point in the winter of 1968 and was accepted by May. I should have been excited and happy. But by the time the acceptance notice came I realized I had applied for West Point because it was what many people expected me to do. For years people had asked, "So, your brothers both went to the Academies...Which one are you going to go to?" Being accepted at one of the Academies became a challenge I could not pass up. So I went through all the tests - mental and physical - and endured the interviews with the conviction I would go to West Point. However, when I received the telegram announcing my acceptance, I had to do a serious analysis of my decision. Much of my interest in West Point had been more of a romantic attachment. I was only fifteen when Fred graduated and had been swept up in the mystique of the place, the uniforms, the parades, and the history.

I turned down the appointment. There were many factors involved in the decision, but the most important was the realization I needed to go in my own direction. My whole life I was the younger sibling of two very successful brothers, and as the son of a gentleman who was known all over town. Whenever I met anyone in Port Huron, the typical question was, "Oh, are you Reed Laughlin's son?" or "Are Gary and Fred your brothers?" It was time for me to find who I was and what I could do as myself.

My parents did not try to influence my decision. Once I decided, they were supportive and offered great encouragement. Years later, they admitted that they did not want me to go to West Point. Mother, especially, was overjoyed when I turned down the appointment. But at the time, they allowed me to make my own decision without parental pressure. Now that I am a parent myself, I realize how hard that must have been. I have always appreciated that about them.

Ultimately I accepted a Reserve Officers Training Corps (ROTC) scholarship at the University of Michigan. The scholarship helped pay for my education and also kept options for the military open, since I had not ruled out doing some military service.

The period from 1968 to 1972 proved to be a particularly difficult time to be a member of any ROTC program. It was criticized and protested on college campuses around the nation. Throughout 1968 and 1969 various government institutions and research centers at the University of Michigan were either bombed or damaged by random fires as the campus became one of the hot-beds of anti-Vietnam War activities. The University's ROTC building was bombed on June 1, 1969 and then seized by student activists on September 22, 1969. Neither the bombing nor the building seizure did significant damage and there were no injuries in either event, but they did initiate a decision by the ROTC staff to change the program and make it less visible on campus. Cadets were not allowed to wear uniforms on campus. The drill and ceremony portion of class was held off campus at a more secure National Guard armory and our military science class requirements were reduced. All this resulted in a more laid back, less military atmosphere in Michigan's ROTC program.

By 1970, and the advent of the draft lottery system, my decision to stay in the ROTC program became a moot point as the first draft lottery was held. The lottery system was based on a random drawing of birth dates. This was supposed to make the draft less subjective, less skewed toward the lower classes, and less biased toward minorities. The order of drawing determined the order of the draft and the likelihood you would be drafted. If your number was less than 200, you would probably get a draft notice when your student deferment ran out. When my draft number was drawn - #68 – I realized I would probably be drafted after college so I might as well stay in ROTC.

That brought me to Fort Lewis in June of 1971. Although this summer camp would substitute for boot camp, it was by no means as strenuous or as demanding as the current experience of boot camp. In 1971 the military had a serious image problem, both on campus and with much of the American public. As a result, the ROTC program did not want to do anything to chase away potential military officers. They were striving for a training program that could prepare us as junior officers without many of the degrading, demanding practices of earlier boot camps. We had our share of early morning wake-ups, unannounced inspections, push-ups, chin-ups, long runs with equipment, and shouting drill sergeants – but we also had frequent breaks, weekend time off, and trips to the officers' club to keep our morale up.

Fort Lewis was the largest military post in the Northwest, located just outside Tacoma, Washington in a beautiful, lush valley dominated to the east by the 14,411 foot high Mt. Rainier. There was a popular saying at Fort Lewis, "If you can see Mt. Rainier - it's going to rain. If you can't see the mountain - it's raining!" Every morning, during our early formation, we could look off and see the mountain - unless, of course it was raining, which it did quite often that summer. We trained rain or shine.

In spite of the wet weather, my decision to come to Fort Lewis in lieu of Fort Riley, Kansas, paid off. We had time off from noon on Saturday until the evening on Sunday, which was plenty of time to rest and regenerate our energy. There was much more to see in the Pacific Northwest than on the plains of Kansas. I tried to take advantage of the location and get out whenever possible. The time off helped develop camaraderie within our unit, as many of us traveled together during our excursions off base. There were cadets from the local area who had driven to camp, so it was easy to get a ride off post. Fond memories and friendships were formed during trips to the Oregon coast, Seattle, and Victoria, British Columbia. The lush green of the forests, contrasted with the deep blue of Puget Sound and the Pacific, and highlighted by the Cascade and

Olympia Mountain ranges, made spectacular scenery for a boy from the Midwest.

On Sunday, June 19, I made my last, and only journal entry while at Fort Lewis. It summed up feelings about the trip and my first impressions of camp. I sent the first part of the journal home to Mom and Dad and gave instructions for them to keep it until I got home. Obviously, they did, since I still have it.

June 19:

Well, I'm a soldier now w/ my haircut, and marching and fatigues, and "Sirs" and weapons and... but I'll never forget my hike. I get rather annoying at times because people ask me about my trip, or say something like "Michigan, wow! What you doing here?" and I start talking about the trip and they can't shut me up! But it sure was great! The sunsets, the roads, the waves, the sands, the mountains, the days and the nights. Little things I'll never forget or be able to explain – like standing under the waterfall at Yosemite, holding an end of a rainbow in each hand. Or the stars at night and the sunrise in Yosemite Valley, or the kid in Westport & the rock hitchhiker there, the dealer in Reno, the cops, other hikers, the Redwoods, Broadway, Golden Gate Park, poison oak, that guy, the seals, being alone, being together, being crowded, missing the crowd, just missing, catching, seeing, looking, wanting, having, loving, winning and losing and loving some more.

So I guess that's about it. One phase of my summer is over and I'm in the middle of my second phase (or should I use the word "life" instead of "phase"). It sure has been great and I could go on here until I run out of pages. But I've become very interested in the feeling back home this summer and very aware of them. And I know they're waiting for this. And I also know I owe more to them for this experience than to anyone or anything else. There is no way I can express the love & feeling I have for all that everyone has given me. I'd like to thank all my riders again and all the people who put me up, but I guess that's impossible. But I can thank the ones I want to thank the most and who I love the most – so THANKS. Thanks for everything and thanks for being you. Guess that's what I love the most. So Thanks. And give my love to all – because I love all.

Also, on June 22 I sent Dad a Father's Day card with a few first impressions of camp:

Home –

First impressions of camp seem very good, have good officers, more time off than expected and OK quarters. Going to lunch in a sec. Went through the confidence (obstacle) course this morning. Beginning to feel all my muscles that weren't there a few weeks ago. Going to throw hand grenades this afternoon. MY BOX CAME YESTERDAY - so now I'm in the process of catching up to everyone else. Still trying to catch up on my journal. I'll try to get it off this weekend. Also have guard duty tonite [sic] from 1:30 - 3:30 (ouch!). Gotta go - give you more later. Happy Father's Day.

Love Tom

Fort Lewis – Making a Team

Most of the cadets at Fort Lewis were from western schools with only a few from east of the Mississippi River. And, of course, no one had hitchhiked across the country to get to camp. This gave me an instant notoriety among my peers and some celebrity in my platoon. Additionally, I stood out because I did not have a full set of uniforms for the first few days. My uniforms, boots, and various military items had not yet arrived at camp. Since it would have been impossible to carry all those items while hitchhiking, I had packed everything in a large box and shipped it to Fort Lewis with the expectation it would be there long before my arrival. However, upon arrival at Lewis, the shipment was nowhere to be found. I was sent all over the post to warehouses and shipping depots to locate it. The box turned up at an off-base UPS storage facility in Tacoma, Washington, where it was being held until claimed. Unfortunately, it took three days to be delivered. During that time I was expected to take part in all the drills and activities. I bought one set of fatigues to get through those first days, but as anyone with military experience can appreciate, without nametags, or any particular insignia, I was subject to considerable harassment from the company officers and my drill sergeant.

Everyone in the military has a story about their first drill sergeant, and I am no exception. My drill sergeant was an interesting example of what the Vietnam War was all about and how it impacted a whole generation of Americans. Drill Sergeant Bell was a college graduate with a degree in economics, but was drafted right after graduation. He had served a year in Vietnam and won medals for bravery and distinguished service. When he came back to the States he became a drill sergeant primarily to avoid further combat. He had no career military plans and was counting the days until he could get out.

He was intelligent, hardworking, and proud of his country. He was also the first Vietnam veteran I met who suffered from Post-Traumatic Stress Disorder (PTSD), although it was not called that in 1971 and was not considered a war related injury until much later. Bell could not attend our training at the mortar range and was absent during our artillery training because the sound of the shells exploding caused flashbacks and disturbed him too much. To us, who considered Drill Sergeant Bell to be tough and strong, the sight of him cowering in fear during the mortar firing exercise was eye opening into the psychological effects of warfare.

Sergeant Bell became a big brother to us – a brother who we both loved and hated, as he pushed us hard, screamed and yelled, insulted, belittled, then complimented you on the great job you had done. He worked us hard, but intelligently, and with a strange amount of humor and compassion. He knew his training would affect our military success, but he also knew he was training a group of college men who were intelligent and motivated to succeed. He would yell and scream at us, then turn around and tell a joke to keep us loose.

When Drill Sergeant Bell first saw me out of uniform, he immediately yelled, "Cadet – what the hell you doing showing up for my formation in civvies? Get your ass in there and get changed!"

"But Drill Sergeant, my uniforms haven't..." I tried to answer.

"Don't give me any excuses! I don't want to hear it."

I immediately became Sergeant Bell's whipping boy. At any time, in those first days before my uniforms arrived, I was subject to his undeniable fury. Even when I did get my box and appeared in uniform, I was subject to his special inspections and treatment to make sure I had caught up with the rest of the troops. Eventually he let up and treated me like the rest of the cadets. I learned a lot about human interaction and coaching from that man.

One particular story illustrates his realization we had to train hard, but realistically. One morning, when we were scheduled for weapons training on the rifle range, it was pouring rain. Of course, nothing was ever cancelled for rain. We proceeded to put on our ponchos – which only made us wetter on the inside – and march out to the range. At the range we had to fire at the targets from the prone position – which meant lying on your stomach in soft sand and trying to hit a target fifty meters away in pouring rain with limited visibility. Being obedient cadets, we got down in the prone position to fire. We discovered we were soon lying in a puddle of water as the rain settled in the low areas around our bodies. Sergeant Bell would then walk up to us and chew us out for lying in a mud puddle and getting the weapon wet.

"Cadet - What the hell are you doing lying in a puddle of water? Didn't your mother tell you to stay out of puddles! You Dumb Ass! Get your scrawny body out of that puddle and finish up!"

Within minutes of relocating we were again surrounded by water and lying in another puddle. Bell would then come back and berate our intelligence for being in the water – all with a smile on his face because he knew nothing could be done about it. The drill sergeant then tried, in his best command voice, to order the rain to stop. He walked up and down the line screaming, "Rain halt!!!" as loud as he could. It got to be such a joke that some of us looked for deeper puddles to try to fire from. Needless to say, no one fired well that day.

I was in the third platoon – the "Third Herd" as we were called. We lived in World War II vintage wooden barracks with lots of little nooks and crannies to collect dust. There were old steam heaters, and exposed wooden rafters throughout. The latrine consisted of a long trough, forty year old toilets, and porcelain sinks with solid brass faucets. We became a close knit group, as all good military units tend to do when they have to depend on each other for success and survival. We were all young college students – intelligent, cocky, and self-confident – and the army seemed to be just a quick stop on our way to success in our future careers. Most of us planned to be teachers, engineers, lawyers, business executives, accountants, bankers, doctors, administrators - anything but career army officers. We worked hard and played hard and stuck up for each other.

Despite all this camaraderie and intelligence, we always failed morning inspections in the eyes of our company First Sergeant. He always found something at fault in his daily inspection of the barracks and made a point of degrading us in front of the whole company. Every day the First Sergeant would inspect and find something - soap scum in the sinks, fingerprints on the faucets, footprints on the floor, dust behind the old radiators, or even dust in the rafters. We would get mad, see it as a challenge, and work harder the next day to pass inspection. We got up earlier and worked to do an extra special job preparing for inspection. The smallest man in the unit was hoisted up to the rafters to wet mop them. We created a tool to dust behind the radiators. We could not use the latrine after 5:30 a.m. so we could shine it up for inspection at 7:00. We buffed the floor twice and everyone double checked their bunkmate to make sure boots were shined, properly placed, and the bunks were made extra tight. Yet we were still the last place platoon in the daily inspection. We realized, as we neared the end of camp, the First Sergeant was always going to put us in last place – not because we were the worst, but to challenge us to do better. That was the army way of teaching teamwork and togetherness – and it worked. We became the best platoon at everything as camp progressed. But of course we still got yelled at.

I discovered the order and structure of military life was a welcome change to my summer. After six weeks of waking whenever, eating whatever, and going anywhere the road took me, I adapted to the regular hours and scheduled routine of the army very well. It created a sense of purpose and mission - which are very important in a military environment. I discovered I enjoyed both lifestyles and was able to easily transition from one to the other.

All military training, regardless of the service, is designed to strengthen you both physically and mentally to prepare for the worst possible conditions during war. This is usually done by depriving the trainee of sleep, food, and emotional support while expecting the ultimate effort physically. At Fort Lewis we trained in the rain and learned to love it. We endured heat and humidity, crawled through the mud, did calisthenics until our muscles ached, went without sleep, stood at attention, ignored bugs, and then did it again – all without question. After all that we went to the classroom and were expected to stay awake, participate and pass all the tests.

You learned to trust your team members and to help your buddy. You made sure your bunkmate was ready for inspection. You helped each other in physical requirements. You became a cheerleader and a decision maker. You let your friend lean on you in formation so he wouldn't collapse from the heat and you learned to succeed together. The end result was a strong, military team – and that was what the army wanted.

We had classroom training designed to teach us the finer points of being an officer in the army - how to fill out paperwork, calculate needs, project training, and all the tedious office jobs that could come along. And, of course, we had plenty of field training. This was the most enjoyable for me, since I much preferred to be outside doing anything. We were given experiences in the various combat branches, with days of infantry, armor, and artillery training. We ambushed, and were ambushed. We drove tanks. We fired howitzers and calculated missile trajectories. A picture of a skinny, fuzz-faced cadet firing a grenade launcher was sent home to the local newspaper saying, "Cadet Laughlin at military training." I guess it was supposed to inspire and reassure the people back home.

We had ranger training and survival training - the culminating exercise being a 48 hour survival test in the wilderness of the Fort Lewis. We had to follow compass coordinates to a certain destination, walk stealthily through the woods throughout the night, surprise the enemy, and move to another location to be picked up by a helicopter. The most memorable part was our dinner. We were given a live chicken and a handful of vegetables to make a stew for our twelve man squad. After killing and gutting the chicken and finding some forest greens to add to the stew we discovered we could make a pretty decent meal. Of course it helped we had not eaten in 24 hours, so anything would have tasted good. After many miles of hiking and completing all the assigned tasks to perfection, we got back to our barracks to again discover we had flunked inspection. So we cleaned everything up, were inspected, and then had a chance to relax for about eight hours before starting all over again.

All of this made the men in our platoon close. We learned who the thinkers were and who the doers were. We learned each man's strengths and weaknesses - which was exactly what all of these situations were supposed to teach us. Many of us stayed close for many years after. I learned lessons that have been valuable throughout the rest of my life - unselfishness, working for the success of the whole and not the individual, and how a group of diverse, intelligent, hard working people can achieve a common goal.

The platoon's success in the physical fitness test was an outstanding example of these lessons learned. The battalion commander issued a challenge to the whole unit. The platoon with the highest average score on the final physical fitness test would win a night at the officer's club with an open bar. That was enough to motivate the Third Herd. We were determined we were going to win the right to drink our fill on the commander's bill.

As the test progressed, I was doing fine – earning the top score of 100 points on all of the challenges except the "hand grenade throw" where you had to throw a grenade into a select target to get 100. Even though I had played baseball my whole life, I was never known for my accuracy and was not able to get over a score of 95 on the grenade throw. As we approached the last event – the two mile run – I knew I could not score a maximum score of 500. I could run the two miles in the required twelve minutes, but it would not change my overall score. But my friend, Bill, had 400 points going into the two mile and could still get a perfect score of 500. However, Bill was a short, squatty offensive lineman from the University of North Dakota who had never been close to the required twelve minute time in his previous training runs. I was determined to help Bill finish in twelve minutes, even if it meant I would not be one of the top runners in the platoon. So I ran with Bill, encouraging him on each lap and keeping him on pace. During the last lap the entire platoon started screaming and yelling for Bill and with all that encouragement, and lots of guts, both Bill and I crossed the finish line in 11:59. The platoon won the challenge and proceeded to have way too much to drink the following night at the officer's club. I was very satisfied. I had not only achieved my personal goal, but had helped my teammate and fellow soldier succeed in something he wanted badly. I felt much greater satisfaction in helping someone else than if I had just gone and run my own race and left Bill to fend on his own.

When graduation day came at the end of July, the Third Herd had evolved into a tight-knit, well run, respected platoon and we won many accolades at the graduation ceremonies. We had become close friends and knew we would have these friendships for many years to come. Most importantly, we knew we could depend on each other for protection and camaraderie if we were ever at war together. We also knew, after passing all the tests thrown at us during camp, we could meet any challenge and come out with flying colors. That's what the army wanted – they had succeeded in their goal of making a bunch of soft college students into intelligent army officers. I realized, even before leaving Fort Lewis, I would never be the same young, naïve twenty-one year old I had been when I arrived there. ROTC boot camp had accomplished its goal.

Near the completion of camp, after a great amount of procrastination, I finally got around to sending my journal home. I included a letter that discussed my feelings about Fort Lewis:

July 12 10:30 PM

Dear Home,

I must apologize [sic] *for taking so long to send this stuff home. I know you're all anxious to read the second leg of my trip and I have been very slow in letting you do this. I had a hard time finishing it up the way I wanted to and saying and remembering everything I wanted to say & felt. It is really quite impossible to get it all down and I guess this thing will never be complete. So much of it will just be said later and never recorded, so here's what I've got so far. Hope you enjoy it and I'll try t answer the questions this will bring up when I get home.*

Talking about getting home – I probably won't be home till late the 29th ('tween 8 & 10 I figure). Might have to hop-scotch across country unless I'm lucky and can get to the airport (30 min. away) by 1:30 & catch a 747 to Chicago. But the General's suppose to talk until 12:00 AND GENERAL'S <u>*NEVER*</u> *get done on time! I'm also going to check into catching a military flight to Selfridge – which would be nice! (But I'm not planning on it!)* [That didn't happen]

We went down to Oregon last weekend. Went to the ocean and just goofed off. Next week we're thinking of going around the Olympia peninsula – we'll do something for sure. Camp is going about like camp goes. Lotsa hard work, but still time for some fun. The more I look around this camp, the more I'm sure I'm in the best platoon of the best Company – not enough room to explain that here. Days are going pretty fast and it will be good to get home.

...Well, I gots [sic] to get to bed. Nice easy day tomorrow, just walk around and look at branch displays. Wed. I'm Plt. Sargant [sic] which could be kinda troublesome. I'll let ya know. So I'll sack out now and try to write a little more, can't promise much though, since next week is gonna be HELL! Anyways, good night.

ALL MY LOVE,
Tom

Publicity photo of me at ROTC Summer Camp.
Pretending to fire an M-79 grenade launcher.

To Europe

"Ladies and Gentlemen, may I have your attention, please. I'm sorry to report that flight 2634 has been delayed for at least another two hours due to mechanical problems. We appreciate your patience, and will keep you informed as flight information becomes available. In the meantime, I'm afraid you will have to remain here in the international departure lounge."

"Noooo!" exclaimed the cute young lady next to me. "Now I'm going to miss my connection. How can I tell my friends in London I won't be there on time? This is terrible."

Similar rumblings came from the crowd all around us. I was mad too, but I tried to keep my cool as I turned to her, "Were you supposed to meet someone in London?"

"Well, yeah. My friends left two days ago and we were supposed to meet tomorrow. We had a couple days in London, and then we're going to Paris. I could not go with them and now I don't know how I'm going to find them."

"Do you know what hotel they are at? Maybe you can call and leave a message."

"Yes, I can probably do that. It just upsets me we are delayed so long. This is our second delay - I'm going to miss half a day in London and I want to see so many things."

"I know - I've got a rather tight schedule myself. But I guess we should just be happy we have the chance to get to Europe. I'm sure it will all work out okay."

"Yeah, I know. Thanks for the reassurance. I'm Sherrie - what's your name?"

"I'm Tom. You a student at Michigan?"

"No, I go to college in Ohio, but live in Grosse Pointe and was able to book this flight. Just finished my sophomore year and I'm taking a month to live with friends outside Paris. I want to improve my French. I'm so excited about it all, I can't wait like this."

"Hey, why don't we sit together on the plane and when we get to London I'll try to help find your friends." Sherrie was a short, petite, brunette with a pleasant smile. It would be much more pleasing to sit next to her than some of the other students I saw in the waiting area.

"That would be great. Thanks for the help."

Thus started the European phase of my summer adventure. It would not be the last delay of the summer, but given my anticipation to leave, it would be one of the most frustrating.

I flew home from Fort Lewis on July 30, right after the graduation ceremony, and started preparing for the final phase of my crazy summer – a twenty-eight day trip around Europe. After arriving home I only had three days to prepare for the trip, so there was very little time to see people, unpack and repack bags, and make final preparations. I had been thinking about traveling through Europe for quite a while, and the timing and circumstances seemed perfect. Of course, my parents and Jackie were upset I was not going to be home longer. I admit it was selfish of me, but looking back I'm glad I did not change anything and was able to squeeze it in.

Upon arrival at Detroit Metropolitan Airport from Seattle, I had an experience that seemed insignificant at the time, but which proved to be life changing. My parents met me at the gate, which I expected (In those days – long before concerns of hijackings, plane bombing, and 9/11 terrorism - friends and family could go right to the gate to meet arrivals). Standing with them was Jackie. She was tan, wearing a short sundress, holding a bouquet of flowers, and looking sexy as she greeted me with a warm kiss and saying how much she had missed me. Although she had written regularly while I was away, I had written very little during the trip west and while at Fort Lewis. This was deliberate because much of the summer I was trying to determine where our relationship was headed and whether or not to continue being with her. We had been dating for over a year and I wanted time to sort things out. I was not sure I was ready for the next step in my commitment to our relationship. Despite my boorish attempt to distance myself, she had been loyal, had written often, and was now standing in front of me looking beautiful. I knew right then this young lady was special.

For the next two days, as I packed for Europe, Jackie patiently helped me prepare and listened to my plans. She seemed excited and supportive of my trip. Throughout my travels in Europe the image of her waiting stayed with me and I realized what a great partner she would be. It would take most of the next year before I asked her to marry me, but I have always felt the day she greeted me at the airport was the turning point in our relationship. We have been together over forty years; she has supported me, and has been my favorite traveling partner.

The plan for the European phase of the summer was simple, at least in my mind. I would fly to England, meet up with friends Mick and Brian - whom I had met the summer before - take a ferry to Sweden to spend time with Thomas, our former exchange student, and then go south into central Europe. In central Europe I would hitchhike and take trains as I circled back to London for the return flight home on the first of September. This portion of the summer would continue to be as inexpensive as possible. Where would I stay? What places would I visit and how far would I go every day? How would I eat or travel or protect myself? No sweat – I planned to make it up on the way. It had worked in the western United States, so why wouldn't it work in Europe?

I was booked on a charter flight through the University of Michigan student services. Smaller, secondary airlines profited by booking flights for college students. They were cheaper than regular airlines, but not famous for their dependability and service. We were told to report to the airport at 1:00 p.m. for a 5:00 p.m. flight. As soon as we arrived there were problems and we were delayed two hours. Mom and Dad had taken me to the airport and when we heard about the delay they took me to lunch. That was my last good meal for the next 24 hours.

After finally checking in, my fellow travelers and I were expected to sit quietly in a small, hot, stuffy, crowded waiting room. Just as we were getting excited about boarding the flight, the attendant announced the second flight delay.

There was very little patience among the passengers. All around me I heard "Let us out of here!"

Someone else yelled, "Get another plane!"

Soon the waiting room was full of disgruntled passengers. "Come on, you can't treat us like cattle!"

I realized it would do no good to add to the comments, so I tried to keep my frustrations to myself and be as patient as possible. More criticism would not help get us in the air any sooner. Besides, I wanted to look cool, calm and unperturbed since Sherrie was next to me.

As the night went on people became more restless, more impatient, and fed up with the airline. Conversely, the airline seemed to not want to hear us and discontinued giving us regular updates on the status of the flight. Finally, about 2:30 a.m. the next morning, they brought in another plane and got us on our way. By this time, most of the passengers had been at the airport for over twelve hours and confined to the small, stinky waiting room for almost ten hours with very little to eat or drink. We were exhausted, frustrated, hungry, and angry. It was not a good way to start the trip.

August 3 – Departure:

Finally got off today about 2:30 AM – Wow – what a hassle! First plane was hurt so we had to wait for another. People sure can show lots of different faces when they have to sit around w/out knowing anything for a whole day. Plane ride was long, crowded and uncomfortable. Got into London about 6:30 PM (London time) – took me two hours to get oriented and find a hostel (1 pound)- Pretty good place – looks like it's going to be all right. Went to a pub tonight – but tomorrow is my day on the town. Phase 4 of my "Summer of summers" has started. Sure hope all goes well.

A Quick Tour of London

We did not get into London until late the next afternoon so the delay wiped out plans for the first day of
sightseeing. Sherrie's friends had learned of the delay,
planned accordingly, and were waiting for her at the
airport. She thanked me for the company on the flight
over, and then disappeared with her friends. We
should have arrived in London in the morning but now
I was a day behind schedule. This was the first in a
series of delays that would prove my schedule to be
idealistic and unrealistic.

One of the important things I learned earlier in the
summer was to pack light. I was much smarter in my
preparation for Europe. This time everything was
squeezed into my small Boy Scout backpack. I wore
one pair of blue jeans, a shirt and a wind-breaker, and
only packed extra underwear, socks, a tee-shirt, a
warmer shirt, and a pair of shorts. I still had my small,
youth sized sleeping bag tied onto the outside of the
backpack but I did not need another bag. This made
traveling much easier.

Upon arriving in London there was only enough time to get a place to stay and look around the local neighborhood. It took a couple hours, but I found a nice youth hostel for the night. There was a light meal at a local pub and a beer to celebrate getting to London. The beer and a good case of jet-lag resulted in a very sound sleep my first night in Europe. I did not realize that, as the summer progressed, getting a full night's rest would become a rarity.

This was my first experience in European Youth Hostels. They had a good reputation for having inexpensive, but clean, accommodation and were popular with both American and European college kids. Most hostels only cost a dollar or two for a night, although some could be more expensive and more elaborate. An international hostel organization monitored the places, but the lodging and rules varied from location to location. It was possible to make reservations at some, but not others. Most of the cheaper ones were on a first come, first served basis. Some of the more expensive hostels had private rooms, but most just provided a large room with bunk beds and group sleeping. Sometimes, for the cheapest rate, you slept on the floor. There were never enough bathrooms.

Since most hostels were first come, first served, they filled up quickly. I was lucky to find a spot so late in London. But I would not get as lucky in other cities as the trip went on. Besides being inexpensive, the best thing about the hostel was a roof over your head and plenty of other young adults in the same situation.

They were friendly, helpful, and would give directions and suggestions of where to travel and where to stay the next night. Overall, the hostel system was perfect for what I wanted to do. My first night in London, on a bunk bed in a large room with twelve to fifteen other youths, was perfect.

My first full day in Europe was a whirlwind tour of London by foot. I met another American college student and the two of us decided to tour together. It was the simplest of adventures, since we did not take any tour busses or use any travel itineraries. We just walked around the central city for about twelve hours and saw as much as possible. We were able to get to most of the standard tourist sites – Westminster, Big Ben, and

Big Ben in London

Trafalgar Square – but the most enjoyment came from just walking the streets of London and being there.

This became a routine during my European tour. There were plenty of young American tourists, most of them trying to see Europe as cheaply as possible. It was easy to spot another American in Europe - they just dressed different and had certain mannerisms that set them apart. Levi's, tee-shirts, and college sweat-shirts were a dead giveaway. You could also tell because Americans usually looked at buildings and people with a curious look of unfamiliarity. I never had a problem meeting new people and my ability to easily talk to people helped.

It was easy to find a traveling companion who was willing to walk and save a few pennies. We would visit the usual tourist stops, but rarely pay. If an entrance fee was required, we would keep on walking. More than anything though, I became fascinated with the different cultures in Europe and often the most enjoyable part of the trip was walking the streets, eating the foods, and learning how people lived in other countries. This leg of my summer trip became a learning experience about the peoples of the world. Thus, London, with its hugely diverse, cosmopolitan atmosphere, became an excellent place to start my European adventure.

August 4:

Saw London today – Westminster Abbey, Big Ben, Trafalgar Square, and all the streets in between. Picca-

dilly Circus is aptly named – "Circus". The people are beautiful. Walked around and got used to pounds. They sure can go fast! Walked around w/a Long Islander until separated.

The Ugly American

Events the next day, August fifth, became symbolic of much of my journey through Europe. I had a pleasant surprise at Buckingham Palace. I saw Sherrie and her friends in the crowd at the changing of the guard and we spent the rest of the day together. She and her four friends made the walk around London more enjoyable. But when the evening came, Sherrie went back to the nice hotel where they were staying, and I returned to traveling solo.

A more significant event was what I called the "Roast Beef and Yorkshire Pudding Controversy". This was my first contact with the "ugly American" syndrome of European travel and the realization America was not always right. In the evening, while walking through the streets of London, I came upon an English pub that was hundreds of years old and famous as the favorite dining spot of many famous English writers, including Dr. Samuel Johnson and Charles Dickens. I decided to give it a try.

"I see that roast beef and Yorkshire pudding is the specialty of the house," I said when my waiter came over. "It's a family favorite my mother has been making for years. Our whole family loves it, so I think I'll have that and see how it compares."

"Good selection sir," my waiter politely remarked. "I think you will be very pleased."

When the order came I discovered the English did not cook it exactly like my mother, which should not have been a surprise. It is never fair to compare something to your mother's favorite dish. But, since the dish originated in England and was the specialty of the house, I figured that was the way it was supposed to be, and I ate the whole thing.

That wasn't the lesson of the day though. Shortly after I arrived, another American couple came in and were seated near me. It was obvious they had a considerable amount of money and were used to getting things done their way. They also ordered the specialty of the house, but when the husband took a bite he loudly called over the waiter.

"This roast beef is terrible! And the Yorkshire pudding is cold. You must take this back to the cook!"

"Yes sir. I'm very sorry. We will bring you a new order immediately," the waiter replied politely.

After a few minutes the waiter brought back another order.

"Thank you," said the American. "This had better be correct or I'll want to speak with the cook."

Well, it did not meet his expectations, and he demanded to see the cook.

When the cook came, the rich American started haranguing him about the quality of his food and the way he cooked roast beef.

"I'm from Texas and we raise our own beef. I know what good beef should taste like and this is like eating shoe leather. English beef is terrible compared to good American beef! You brag about being the home of roast beef and Yorkshire pudding and you serve us this crap! I can't believe you expect us to pay these prices. This is terrible..." He proceeded to dress down the cook in front of the whole restaurant. The poor man never had a chance to respond.

"Come on. We're getting out of this place," he said to his wife and got up and walked out without paying for his drinks or the meals.

When things quieted down I realized what he had really accomplished by his demonstration was to make himself, and other Americans, look arrogant, conceited, and demanding. I thought to myself, *This is the home of roast beef and Yorkshire pudding! They have made it here for hundreds of years. Maybe we Americans are the ones who don't know how it's supposed to taste.* I resolved to try as many local foods as possible while in

Europe and not prejudice my opinions with thoughts of what it would taste like at home.

This rude American became the epitome of what was wrong in international relations on a small, personal scale. Americans were demanding the rest of the world listen to them, insisting they were right and the rest of the world was wrong. Even though other countries had successes and opportunities to offer everyone, many Americans felt they were the number one nation and therefore were always right. In a small way, I started viewing the role of America in world affairs in a different manner after that minor incident in a London restaurant. That evening seemed to symbolize much of what was wrong in the world.

That night I slept in the Euston Station railroad terminal. I was taking an early train north to Chester and it was much cheaper and easier just to sleep in the waiting area. Train stations became a common overnight stop for me. The stations always had people around, including police, so were relatively safe. You usually had to sleep sitting up in a chair, but if you could find a quiet, out of the way place to lay on the floor you could get some real sleep. True, you had to sleep on the hard floor, and sometime during the night the cleaning crew would come and make you move – but it was free, warm, and dry. Some stations allowed travelers to sleep as long as they were in one particular area, while others forced you to move every hour and threatened to arrest you for loitering. This first experience in Euston Station was good – I got some sleep and made my morning train – but others would not be so pleasant.

August 5:

Post Office Tower and the Monument Tower of London – more streets, more people – Sherrie and Co. and Roast Beef and Yorkshire Pudding. (Yours is better Mom!) Spent the night in Euston Station on the floor. Tourists are tourists the world over except they get more of them here. Ages of things here fascinate me – 3, 4, or 5 hundred years old – or 1000!

Wales, the Lake District & Scotland

My first impression of Great Britain outside of London came while riding the train to Mick's home in Chester, England. I had met Mick, an Englishman, and Brian, a Scotsman, the previous summer at Camp Greylock for Boys in the Berkshire Mountains of Massachusetts. The camp was a month long, sports oriented, overnight camp for boys. We had been hired for a six week period as camp counselors and coaches. When camp ended we traveled to Washington D.C. together and became good friends. We exchanged addresses and promised to keep in touch. In the spring, as my summer plans started coming together, I wrote them and said I would like to visit. I had a vague idea of when I would be arriving, but nothing specific. I just told Mick I would call when I got to Chester. Hopefully he would be ready for me.

Today, with the advent of instant communications by email and cell phones, coordinating my trip and arrival times with Mick and Brian would be easy. But that was not possible in 1971.

There is no greater change in the last forty years than those in the area of communications. The communication revolution was brought on by an amazingly rapid advance in technology for mass media and the individual. Years from now history books will look at the changes that occurred as a result of computers, the internet, and cell phones. These and other changes have made worldwide communications affordable and instantaneous. Those changes have created a revolution around the world impacting, politics, economics, culture and society.

These changes have made world leaders more responsive to the demands of their citizens, as seen by the Arab Spring of 2012, when protests and demonstrations caused the collapse of autocrats and dictators throughout the Middle East. These protests were coordinated with the use of cell phones and social media. In the Sixties and Seventies word of an upcoming protest would take days to organize, since people could only be notified by word of mouth, hand-outs, or telephone calls. Today a protest can be set-up within minutes. Years ago political opinions were given in speeches and in newspapers. Today politicians use the internet and social media to increase their exposure to their electorate.

The economics and business spheres have been quick to use new technology and communications to provide products and services cheaper, faster, and with higher quality than ever before. The major corporations in the world are linked by a worldwide communications system that produces jobs and economic prosperity for everyone. These methods of rapid communications were only a dream as I watched the British countryside whiz by. I would just have to trust the fates to help me connect with Mick once I arrived in Chester.

As my train sped along I saw well maintained and prosperous looking British farms surrounding small villages that looked as if they had come from a tour book. I did not see junk yards, empty warehouses, or abandoned fields - which was what always seemed to be near American rail lines. Everything was on time and orderly. Rail travel in Great Britain was impressive, since there was nothing like it in the States. The train was fast, smooth, and efficient. I had traveled by train at home, but it did not have the same comfort or timeliness as the British Railway. It struck me as one more thing America could improve on.

I called Mick as soon as I arrived in Chester, and thankfully he was prepared. He picked me up at the station and gave me a tour of Chester – its Roman ruins, medieval town center, and of course the English pubs. The pubs quickly became a favorite spot - not only because of the delightful flavor of the local ale, but also because of the low-key, casual atmosphere. Mick was intelligent, personable and very knowledgeable of his hometown. He seemed to know every interesting spot and all the key individuals in the places I wanted to see. We stopped at Mick's favorite pub and the local patrons soon befriended his Yankee guest. In no time they had me drinking and singing with the greatest impromptu quartet and playing darts against a guy who bragged of being the dart champion of Chester. Of course my singing was lousy and I lost at darts - but they did not care. They welcomed me in spite of my shortcomings.

August 6:

On rail to Mick's – Beautiful, beautiful countryside. Train is great, too. Goes up to 100-110 MPH and had the best breakfast and service of anywhere. Looks like a great day!

The next morning we drove south into Wales to visit Mick's girlfriend. This was a quiet, relaxing day of driving and enjoying an afternoon in the country. The Welsh scenery of small towns, beautiful rolling hills, and lush green valleys impressed me. The best part of the day was that I was not a tourist as much as a friend

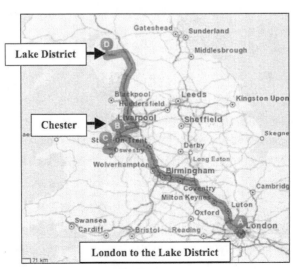

taking part in the everyday activities of Mick and his family. The hospitality of Mick and his friends made me feel comfortable and relaxed in their presence.

The following day Mick and I drove to the Lake District of England and hiked the third tallest mountain in England, Mt. Hellvellyn. It was not a strenuous climb – it had a well marked path and a gentle incline – and after all the walking and fitness training done at boot camp it was an easy challenge. The view from the top was worth it. The lakes and small mountains that made the area famous were displayed below us in all their grandeur. Then it was on to the home of poet William Wordsworth, and a relaxing afternoon in one of the most beautiful parts of the British Isles. For the first time, the Romantic poetry of the 19th century I studied in college started to make sense. When surrounded by the pristine lakes and ancient peaks of northwestern England it was easy to see why Wordsworth, Coleridge and others would write about the beauty of nature and man's peace and solitude in the environment.

The next day we headed north to Scotland and my immersion in British history continued with a stop at Hadrian's Wall - the ancient dividing line between the Roman world of southern Britain and the Picts in the north. I realized I had visited historical sites spanning 2000 years of western civilization and had only traveled a couple hundred miles. Nothing similar could be experienced in North America.

On top of Mt Hellvellyn

We arrived at Brian's apartment in Edinburgh in the afternoon and surprised him by being earlier than anticipated. Brian Samson was a short, solidly built 22 year old Scotsman who had come to the United States as a soccer and rugby coach. He attended university classes in Edinburgh and lived in a small apartment in town. He was not expecting us until later and was preparing to go to rugby practice when we arrived. He started to excuse himself, but I surprised him by asking if I could join him.

"I'd love to join you if you wouldn't mind," I said. "I'd like to compare training methods between Scotland and the U.S. and I could work out a little on the side."

"Know anything about rugby?" Brian asked.

"The basics – my brother played rugby at West Point and I saw a few matches. It's a great game."

"Then come on, let's go."

I joined Brian at his practice and watched from the sidelines and noted the similarities of warming up, pregame preparations, and game planning. It reminded me of any other sport I had been involved in.

"Hey Tom," Brian yelled, "We're short a man, can you fill in?"

Feeling a little humble, but honored they would ask, I was compelled to join the contest.

"Just play out on the wing, and don't get hurt," the team captain said.

"Yeah, that's fine. I've played American football my whole life, so I should be okay," I said, trying to sound knowledgeable and confident.

"Well Yank – just be sure you don't tackle like they do in the States. You don't have a helmet in this game, so you can't put your head in front. Put it to the side and you'll be fine."

"Okay – don't worry about me," I said cockily.

The first few minutes went fine and I was just getting the hang of the game when my big chance came.

The opposing team was on the move and the runner was right in front of me, so I did what came naturally - put my head down and went for the good American form tackle. And, of course, the runner did what every Scotsman is trained to do in rugby - picked his knees up and smacked me right in the side of the head.

Next thing I remember is laying on my back and looking up through blurry eyes at Brian and the team captain.

"You okay Yank? I told you not to put your head in first when you tackled," laughed the captain.

With that, I retired to the sidelines and nursed a splitting headache through the rest of practice. The Scots were good sports though. They invited me to their post-practice pub stop, had some good laughs at my expense, and even paid for the beer. The beauty of sports is that the camaraderie and joy of competition is a universal feeling and does not know international boundaries.

I loved the history, culture, and food of England and Scotland. I promised myself to return in the future for a more thorough visit. Being with Mick and Brian allowed me to live with the locals and not feel like a tourist. I learned about their schools, jobs, families, and how the average Englishman and Scotsman spent their days. These were parts of their lives I would not have seen otherwise.

August tenth was a day for a quick tour of Edinburgh - the castle, Royal Mile, and of course more Scottish pubs. That night, while discussing things at Brian's, I realized I had a serious problem. The original plan had been to go south from Edinburgh to Dover, cross the English Channel, then proceed either by train or hitchhiking to Sweden to meet Thomas. Somehow, in my inexperience of European travel, I thought I could do that in two or three days.

I had written Thomas before I left the States and told him I would meet him at his family home in Lindesberg, Sweden, on August twelfth. Thomas and his girlfriend, Marianne, were leaving Lindesberg on August thirteenth to move to southern Sweden. Thomas had been hired for a teaching position in the town of Falkenberg and had to get moved in. However, as I sat at Brian's and looked at train and ferry schedules, I realized there was no way I could get to Lindesberg on time. It was much further than anticipated and the trains did not run as regularly as I had imagined. I did not have a phone number for Thomas or his family, thus communication with them was impossible. I would have to go to Lindesberg and keep my fingers crossed. Thus began an interesting race to try to catch my Swedish friends before they moved.

Mike and Brian decided my best bet would be to try to catch the first ferry from England directly to Sweden. The next day Mick drove me south to the port city of Newcastle on Tyne to catch the ferry, but we missed the boat by thirty minutes. At that point I was committed to the ferry route, and the next possible connection was an overnight ferry to Bergen, Norway. This put me even further behind schedule. From Bergen I would take a train through Norway and into Sweden and try to catch Thomas. I thought this could be done in less than two days and I could get back on schedule. Of course, I did not have a copy of a Norwegian train schedule and none of us knew how long the trains in Norway and Sweden would take. I would find that out later. Since I could not communicate this time problem to Thomas, I had to proceed and hope for the best. My, how things have changed.

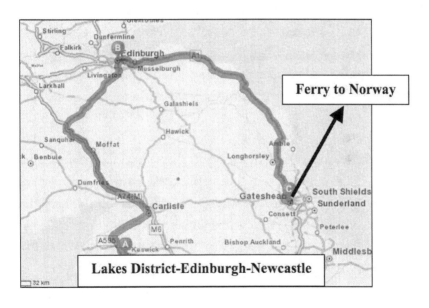

Today we can see fashions, art, entertainment, and tragedy anywhere in the world as it is happening. Young people traveling in Europe, like I did in 1971, can call home on their cell phones with very little difficulty. They can access the internet almost anywhere in the world to email letters to friends and relatives, then check airplane and train schedules and even buy the tickets online. They can transfer money from bank accounts if they need to. But that is today, not the world I was traveling in back then.

In 1965, when Thomas was living with my family in Michigan, he almost forgot how to speak Swedish when his parents surprised him with a telephone call at Christmas time. It had been over four months since he had spoken his native language or talked to his parents and he could not think of the Swedish words to say. Today, exchange students in the U.S. frequently call or email their parents every day. Today a person can receive an email notification of airline delays or traffic problems. Communications are quick, easy, and inexpensive. This was unimaginable forty years ago.

In 1971 it was possible, but difficult and expensive, for the average person to make international telephone calls. Even domestic long-distance phone calls were charged by the minute for each call and could become expensive if your call went over five or ten minutes. For me to communicate with Thomas in Sweden would have involved either a letter which would take up to a week to arrive, a telegram which would cost ten to twenty dollars, or a telephone call that would again cost ten to twenty dollars. I learned it was usually best to go ahead with plans that were made and hope for the best. My philosophy was to adjust when I got there if the plans did not work out. Little did I know how much my philosophy would be challenged while traveling through Scandinavia trying to meet my Swedish brother.

August 14:

Now on rail on the way to Oslo, then Thomas [in Sweden]. It's been some time since my last entry and a lot has happened. Mick and Brian were great to me and the English in general were very nice – in their own way. I've tried to appreciate the way the people over here live and not complain about difference in customs, habits, food, etc. You can never "learn" a country if you want and expect everything to be like home (I must say – Mom's cooking sure is good – espec. roast beef and Yorkshire pudding!) But it's more fun that way and I have had fun. I'm behind schedule – didn't plan on being in Eng. so long, but it was worth it – even if I can't see all I wanted to. Just have to see.

In the Hall of the Mountain King

I bid farewell to Mick at the station and settled back for an overnight ferry ride across the North Sea to Bergen, Norway. Since the ferry was leaving at 10:00 p.m., I planned to find a comfortable spot and sleep on the boat in order to be well rested when I got to Norway. But that did not work out. The North Sea is famous for being unpredictable and having rough weather and that night was no exception. As the ferry cleared the harbor the wind and waves picked up. The ship was a typical car ferry – wide and with a blunt bow which made it ride high on every wave. Within an hour of putting out to sea the ship was being violently rocked up and down. Even the crew said it was one of the worst seas in quite a while. No one could sleep and most of the passengers became seasick. Although I did not get seasick, I got very little sleep during the passage.

I was rewarded the following morning, with a calm sea and brilliant sunrise as we made our way into the Bergen Fjord. I had seen many tourist posters and postcard pictures of the Norwegian fjords, but seeing them in person was even more impressive. The water was deep blue, crystal clear and glistening in the sunlight. For the second time in the summer a beautiful sunrise offered great hope for the future. The mountains rose directly from the water's edge to awesome heights with sheer cliffs and long, misty waterfalls coming out of crevices. The view took my breath away. This was by far the most memorable landscape of the entire summer.

Bergen was a pleasant diversion from the original plans. Unfortunately the schedule became more disrupted because the only train to Oslo left very early in the morning, and the ferry did not arrive until mid-morning. I could not believe there was only one train to Oslo, and I also did not realize how far Bergen was from Oslo, since you had to cross the ridge of the Norwegian mountain chain. So, I was stuck in Bergen for the rest of the day, which added one more delay in my attempt to catch up with Thomas.

Bergen was a delightful city, and a very pleasant spot to be stranded. It was isolated, but up to date. It was deep in history, yet very modern. It was proudly Norwegian, but also worldly cosmopolitan. It was endowed with culture and music was everywhere. There were musicians on the street corners, parks with small orchestras playing music, and museums to classical music - in particular the music of Edvard Grieg. Bergen was Grieg's hometown and many of the activities were focused on his music. I had never listened to much classical music, but I was familiar with Grieg, in particular his piece *In the Hall of the Mountain King*, which was most appropriate to the surroundings. It was a warm summer day so I enjoyed wandering around town, visiting the fishing docks, and resting in a beautiful park while a small group of musicians played Grieg. That night I bought my ticket for the morning train to Oslo and slept in the station.

The ride to Oslo took over eight hours. The train stopped at many small Norwegian villages, but the beauty of the mountains and the quaintness of the villages made the slow pace worthwhile. I could be a tourist without leaving the train. There was always something to see outside the windows - local women boarding the train to shop in the next small village, men in their work clothes traveling down the tracks ten or fifteen miles to their fields, even children using the train to get to school. It made the progress slow, but interesting. The train wound its way up the Norwegian mountain chain then slowly made its way down to Oslo. I slept, relaxed and enjoyed the beautiful countryside.

Along the way I met a couple of fellow travelers – two young men from New Jersey. They were talking to two beautiful Norwegian girls who spoke excellent English. Olga and Elizabeth looked like they had just come off a poster advertising the beauties of Scandinavia. They were both eighteen, tall, and personable, with very shapely, buxom figures. Olga, in particular, caught my eye. She had big, bright blue eyes, a beautiful smile, and an easy, relaxed manner around strangers. I had to join in the conversation just to have an opportunity to sit and admire her beauty. As the day went on we talked more and decided to stick together when we got to Oslo.

We arrived late that evening and immediately tried to book a room at the youth hostel near the train station. I discovered one important aspect of getting into hostels – it was easier if a native traveler helped out. Officially the hostel was full, but after Olga flashed her smile and talked to the desk clerk she convinced him we could all stay together in one room and sleep on the floor. While that may sound a little kinky, it turned out we were in a large room with four or five other travelers and did, in fact, sleep on the floor. One small fantasy did come true though – and a revealing example of the cultural differences between Norway and the States – when my beautiful lady friends decided it was time to go to sleep. They walked over to the other side of our darkened room and, silhouetted against the wall, pulled off their tops and bras, pulled on a tee-shirt and took off their pants. Then, in a very uninhibited manner, they came over and sat down in front of us and continued their conversation before we all crawled into our sleeping bags for the night. To them it was no big deal, but I could not see that happening in the States without making a scene. The calm and comfort they felt in stripping down to their underwear made me realize it was generally accepted in their world. I could get used to that.

The next morning I was up early and on the first train to Sweden. Thus began a two day expedition through Sweden to rendezvous with Thomas. I was supposed to be in Lindesberg, Sweden, Thomas's family home, by August twelfth. However, I was already more than a day behind schedule and I had not talked, or written, to Thomas in almost a month. There was no direct train from Oslo to Lindesberg, so I had to take a train to Goteborg, transfer to Orebro, then get a local train to Lindesberg. This took the whole day and I did not arrive in Lindesberg until early evening on the fourteenth. Thomas and Marianne had waited as long as they could before leaving the day before to move to Falkenberg, on the southwest coast of Sweden. The next twenty-four hours would be an amazing example of Swedish hospitality and family togetherness.

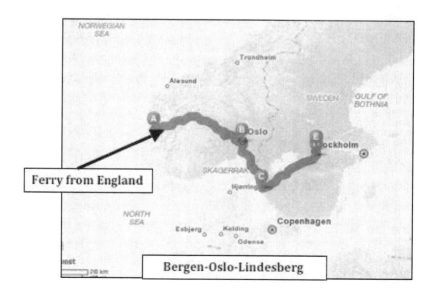

Ferry from England

Bergen-Oslo-Lindesberg

April 14: continued

Norway is amazing. Glad I came this way, although it is very expensive (finished off my first $100 today – that's about an $8.00/day average.) But the land is beautiful – so rugged and tough. You get the feeling and awe of the early people –the Norsemen. As Thomas said, "Those Wikings [sic] were hard people!" They had to be. In Eng. and Scotland I was impressed w/the age of everything. The castles, the Roman walls, everything has history behind it and is old. In Norway it's rough, lonely and starkly beautiful. Plain and simple but beautiful. This is obviously a land of legend and folklore. You can see it. Where Eng. was a land of history – Norway is the land of trolls and elves. And it's all a storybook world!

A Scandinavian Rendezvous

The experience of being a foreigner in a foreign land can intimidate any traveler, but the Swedish people generated so much friendliness that any fear or intimidation was quickly diminished. Thomas had always bragged about how friendly Swedes were, and I discovered he did not exaggerate at all. It began with the conductor on the train to Lindesberg. When the train arrived in Orebro I only had a few minutes to transfer to the train for Lindesberg. I had not had time to exchange currency and only had Norwegian krone. The conductor looked at me, looked around, then quietly said, "That's okay - just stay here."

That was great, but upon arrival in Lindesberg, I had an address, but no idea where the Kierkegaard home was.

"Do you speak English?" I asked a young boy. Most Scandinavians did, but I always asked to be polite. "I need help finding this address," and showed him the address.

"Sure - Come with me. I'll take you there," and this boy of about twelve led me through the streets for a half mile to the Kierkegaard home. I kept telling him he did not have to take me all the way, but he insisted. He said it was his way of welcoming me to their little town.

I knocked on the door, but no one was home. Dejected, I sat on the porch and pondered my next step.

"Nils will be home in about an hour," Mr. Kierkegaard's neighbor said looking over the fence at me. "Can I help you?"

"Well, thank you, but I'll just wait for Mr. Kierkegaard to get home."

"Come on over and have a cup of coffee. There is no sense waiting by yourself."

The neighborly attitude prevailed, and I ended up talking to them for over an hour before Thomas's father came home.

When Thomas' father arrived the first thing he did was call Thomas and tell him I was okay and in Lindesberg. Thomas was already about 300 miles to the south in Falkenberg, so we had to arrange how we were going to get together. Nils said not to worry; he would take care of everything. He then fixed an outstanding supper (Thomas' mother had died some years before, so Nils did it all), offered me some of his prized, homemade schnapps, and arranged transportation for me.

The next day Thomas' sister and her husband drove me over 200 miles south, while Thomas and Marianne drove north to our rendezvous. They continued the amazing family attitude of kindness and refused any payment for the ride.

Throughout my stay in Sweden and Norway I was in awe of the openness and kindness of the people. They went out of their way to help make me comfortable. While the scenery and landscapes were spectacular, it was the people I remember most from my brief journey through Scandinavia. I could not have made it without them.

Thomas and Marianne were a young couple – each 23 years old – just starting out in new jobs. Both were employed as physical education teachers, and although they were not married yet, were sharing an apartment in town. They were moving in, so much of my time was helping them get situated and getting to know the city along with them. It was great to be able to do normal things with Thomas – move furniture, paint walls, and hang pictures – instead of being a tourist.

The next day Thomas had to visit his new school, so I went along and toured the gymnasium - as they called high school – where he would be teaching. As the son of two teachers and a future teacher myself, I wanted to compare schools, equipment, and programs. I was very impressed with the modern facilities and the Swedish curriculum. I was a bit envious of Thomas at that point in his life. He was settled, had a new job, a beautiful and personable girlfriend, and was excited about his future. In contrast, my future seemed uncertain and subject to a lot of outside forces I could not control.

August 21:

Broke down and bought a pen – so maybe I can catch up a little. On the train from Copenhagen to Lubeck, Germany. Good train.

Oslo – didn't see much but met some great kids. Got into practice catching trains.

Finally found Thomas – ended up as a chase all over Sweden. Thomas had gone to Falkenberg to meet me and I went to Lindesberg. Feel very bad because I inconvenienced so many people. Nevertheless, they gave me the royal treatment. Everyone in Sweden was wonderful to me. The land of Sweden was very nice (and "naturally" there was lots of sun!). The land was kind of unique land, but the beauty of Sweden is not its land – but its people. The people of Sweden are just beautiful. Not only physically – like the girls – but all the way around. People, like the conductor who let me go from Orebro to Lindesberg for free because I didn't have any Swedish Krone. Or the kid who walked a half mile with me when I asked for directions and would have gone all the way to T.K's [Kierkegaard's] house if I hadn't said something. Or the neighbor who took me in when no one was home. These were the people and they were always smiling and willing to help.

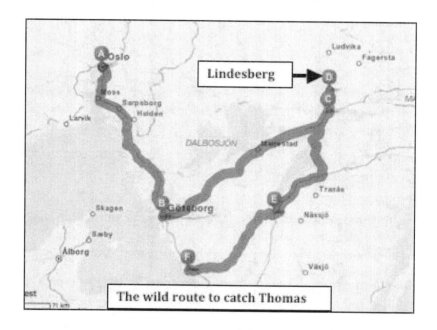

The wild route to catch Thomas

An Evening Conversation

It was while helping Thomas and Marianne move into their apartment that I realized, with a little patience and understanding, the people of the world could communicate even without knowing one another's language. Thomas had some friends help move heavy furniture and after getting things moved, ordered pizza and brought out beers. His friends spoke English to me, but Swedish amongst themselves. Since the others were speaking Swedish - which I did not speak - I sat back in a corner, ate my pizza, and relaxed. Suddenly I found myself laughing at something that was said.

Thomas looked up, saw me laughing, and said, "Did you understand that?"

"Well, I think so...He was talking about his girlfriend, how they had gotten into an argument, then had a romantic night of making up. Or something like that..."

"That's exactly right," said Thomas. "How did you know?"

"I guess it was just the body language, the inflection of his voice, and the whole situation. I could imagine the same conversation happening back home."

We all had a good laugh and I realized things were not much different even though I was thousands of miles from home.

As the evening went on, Thomas's friends sat down and we started talking politics and America's international image. When the subject of Vietnam came up Thomas asked, "I thought you would be strongly in favor of your country's involvement over there. Don't you have to go into the army?"

"Yes, I do. This time next year I'll be a second lieutenant in the army. I'm excited about that - I like the idea of travel and the physical challenge of the army - but I'm not excited about going to Vietnam. I think about it all the time. I have some concerns about the whole thing. I don't really like the war, but realize I will probably have to go. If I do, I will go with a firm commitment to do my job. That's the problem a lot of my army friends are facing. We don't really like it, but we know we have to do the best we can do."

"Why doesn't the U.S. get out of Vietnam?" they asked. "From what we see on our news, it looks like everyone in America is protesting the war. But your politicians keep talking about defeating North Vietnam. From our viewpoint, it doesn't make sense."

"Well, it's complicated and hard to explain." I said. "We are a proud nation. Our military has a tradition of success. We don't want to look weak to the rest of the world." But, when I said that, they all started to laugh.

"That pride is hurting the U.S. Why are you so worried about looking weak? To Europeans, the U.S. looks bossy, domineering, and stupid. You are trying to do too much and are looking like Big Brother to the rest of the world. Staying involved in Vietnam is hurting the image of America more than getting out ever would."

Lars, the most politically savvy and outspoken of the group, said, "I do not understand the bickering and name calling of your political parties. They can't seem to agree on anything. Why don't they agree the war and economy are important problems that need to be solved?"

That made me think. I was proud of being an American and treasured the rights and freedoms we enjoyed. I was willing to fight to protect those if necessary. But I had always looked at America's involvement from our own perspective and now I was being confronted with an international viewpoint I had never thought about. Thomas and his friends had some good points and opened my eyes. Maybe we were not always right.

Lars continued, "What I really don't understand is why the United States – the richest and most powerful country in the world – doesn't take better care of its citizens. I mean, you have too many poor, you don't provide health care, and you don't take care of your old! Here in Sweden our government takes care of us. Why won't your government take care of you that way?"

"Wow – good observations." I said. "But in America we practice capitalism and hate the idea of socialism. To most Americans everything you described is socialistic and would get the government too involved. The American way is that if you are down, you work hard and make more money to pay for what you need. Besides, Americans hate high taxes and we know here in Sweden, and other socialized nations, you pay very high taxes."

"Well, I pay about 45% of my income as a teacher in taxes, and it could get higher as I get older and make more money," said Thomas. "But I get a lot back for that. We don't have to pay for anything from cradle to grave. Medical care, old age pensions, even unemployment if that comes along, is all paid for. I will have child care leave of up to one year when Marianne has a baby. Our education is free, all the way from pre-school through university training. I do pay high taxes, but I think it's worth it."

Lars added, "We have socialistic policies to care for our people, but we are just as capitalistic as anyone. We all want to get rich, and Sweden gives us plenty of opportunity to do that. We have a democratically elected government that protects our rights and freedoms. Isn't that what Americans are always bragging about? I don't see how your system is any better than ours."

"Well, you make a good argument, but I don't know if America will ever go along with that. Anything that sounds like socialism or communism seems to push a panic button in most Americans. The fear of socialism would be a major obstacle to making those changes. I don't see the U.S. ever getting to that point."

The conversation changed to lighter topics and the evening wound down, but the thoughts and opinions of my new Swedish friends made me think. Why was America against anything that sounded socialistic? Why could not we have a variation of their socialized medicine? Why didn't our government do more for the poor and unemployed and disabled? Why were we so afraid of higher taxes? If we expect our government to provide services for us – even basic things like a strong military, good police, good urban infrastructure – we had to pay for it. Our federal income tax was not as high as Sweden's, but we had other taxes hidden in the cost of products. Federal income taxes may be 28% or higher. State income taxes varied, but could range from 4% to 10%. And then there was the vast assortment of city taxes, sales taxes, property taxes, gas taxes, and even luxury taxes. Maybe Americans were paying almost the same amount as Swedes after paying all those taxes. Maybe their system was not as scary as the American media and politicians made it out to be. It worked in Sweden and a lot of other European nations – why couldn't it work for ours?

Much of that conversation is still appropriate forty years later. True, Vietnam is no longer the topic of discussion, but in many ways America's overseas image, political partisanship, and distaste of government involvement have not changed. We have a more globalized economy, but still struggle with our political image overseas. Of course, we still need to think of what is best for the United States in foreign affairs, but we also need to work in conjunction with other nations and look at the issue from a global perspective. We can no longer commit an act in isolation. In an interdependent, globalized world, our actions affect everyone's political, economic, and social life. Being a world leader means we need to be more aware of our international image.

We can still learn from other countries. We are still looking for ways to provide better medical care for U.S. citizens, but Americans still have hesitation with the idea of a government run medical system. We have made very little progress in providing for our poor, disabled, and unemployed in the last forty years. The gap between rich and poor is greater than ever. Our education system and urban infrastructure have not improved and many consider them to be worse. In many ways America has remained at status quo while the rest of the world has progressed. We need to study what they have done right and what has worked for them and apply those lessons here.

Let's be more international, more global, and more concerned in the future.

Europe: Then and Now

The Europe of 1971 was vastly different from today's Europe. There were still scars left from World War II, even though it had ended over 25 years earlier. The most obvious was the geographical split created by the division of Germany into West and East Germany and the undeniable impact of the Iron Curtain on European life. The Capitalist vs. Communist split, the West vs. the East, and the ramifications of the Cold War were everywhere – not just in Germany. The political leaders of every major nation were members of the World War II generation and their political decisions were influenced by the actions and decisions made before, during, and after the war. There were still nationalistic prejudices amongst the people – Germans not liking the French, and vice versa; bitterness from the Dutch and Belgians; conflict between Germans and Poles; and many other subtle antagonisms often came up in discussion.

As my conversation with my Swedish friends illustrated, Europeans were very interested in international events, especially those involving the United States. They were not directly involved in the Vietnam conflict but followed it closely and had strong opinions about what was happening. Europeans knew any conflict or treaty between the United States and the Soviet Union would somehow impact them. They were aware Europe was a major battle site on the war plans of both super-powers. Consequently there were large anti-war and anti-nuclear organizations throughout Europe.

It was a time of uncertainty and concern amongst Europeans, but it was also an exciting time with new industries starting up, new economic powers developing, and new beginnings for the younger generation of Europe. Like the youth movement in the U.S., the youth of Europe wanted more rights, freedoms, and opportunities. They did not want to be bound by the same restrictions as their parents' generation. They protested for more educational freedoms, more social mobility, and more voice in their governments. They had seen the destruction of war more than Americans. In many ways they were more revolutionary than the American youth counter-culture. Whereas the American counter-culture had read about, and intellectually studied, the effects of war, communism, and old political systems, the youth of Europe had lived through them and had seen their impact first hand. Whenever I spoke with European youth – whether in England, Sweden, Germany, France, or the Netherlands – the concerns and feelings about war and peace were the same.

The Common Market - which provided tariff free trade between six western European nations (Belgium, the Netherlands, Luxemburg, Italy, France, and West

Germany) - was just beginning and still in its experimental stage. The idea of a European Union and a universal currency were dreams for the future. Each nation closely protected its borders, imposed tariffs and taxes on certain goods, and had its own currency whose value ebbed and flowed every day depending on the market. The physical divide between the communist and the free nations – as demonstrated by the Berlin Wall and the vast fortified and fenced borders running from the Baltic to the Mediterranean – was going to be there forever and the thought of it coming down was left to dreamers. In the eyes of most, there would never be a unified Europe – but that was okay because everyone was proud of their ethnic and national heritage and accomplishments.

One of the most interesting things I noticed while traveling from one country to the next were the ethnic differences between the peoples of Europe. Englishmen could differentiate between an Englishman and a Scotsman. Swedes knew if someone was from Norway or Denmark, even though they all looked the same to me. Germans and Frenchmen may have lived only a few miles apart, but their dress, food, and even housing styles could be much different. These ethnic differences were a source of pride among many Europeans, but it also created many conflicts and prejudices. Ethnic pride was a much more important part of their society than in the United States and many Americans had a difficult time understanding its significance in European lives. It impacted everything from food, clothing, and culture - but most importantly, it influenced the political thoughts and decisions of Europeans. It could isolate people or bring them together. It was key to the traditions and heritage of a nation. Today those ethnic differences and barriers are slowly breaking down, but it will take time before they change or disappear.

Traveling through Europe was different in 1971 than it is today. Although I could get by without speaking the native language, there was much less English spoken than today. The French, in particular, had a reputation for being rude and impatient to anyone who did not speak fluent French, and they were proud of that reputation. Trains and busses stopped at the border and sometimes you had to change trains to the rail system of the new nation. Every nation had its own unique monetary system and you needed to exchange currency at the border. It was complicated and inconvenient.

The development of the European Union (EU) - which now stretches from Great Britain east to the borders of Russia - has made Europe politically and economically much different today. The political union is still in its infancy and struggles to get wide acceptance as people want to protect their national identities and traditions. Economically, the EU has been much more successful and is now the third largest economic block in the world. Trade is conducted without tariffs and commercial transportation links the European business world. The Euro is the common currency and simplifies financial dealings among EU nations and their citizens. For all its economic success, however, there remains a huge disparity between the rich and poor nations which has caused some financial instability.

For the foreign traveler, the creation of the European Union is a vast improvement and has made traveling in Europe much easier. There are no border checkpoints or passport inspections when traveling within the EU. Having a common currency means travelers do not have to worry about exchanging currency and fluctuating values. Also, Europeans have taken full advantage of the improvements brought on by the Communications Revolution. Europe is crisscrossed by internet and cell phone communications. The flow of both commercial and personal business is smooth and efficient today.

English is spoken almost everywhere - with the younger generation leading the way. While there is still considerable nationalistic pride and partisan politics throughout the European nations, there is also much more cooperation in international matters. The political leaders of today are often successful businessmen or members of the Baby Boom generation who did not live through the events of World War II. And, in perhaps the biggest change of the last forty years, the communist world of Eastern Europe is now broken up, open to the rest of the world, and part of the European Union and NATO.

In 1971 Europe was still vibrant with history and culture and that was what I wanted to experience. It was exciting for me to learn about a particular place, building, or region's history. Who settled there? What was its historical significance? What happened at this place and who did it? Even the smallest villages seemed to have something to pique my curiosity. The clean efficiency of Scandinavian towns and the red tiled roofs of the German villages had a unique charm and attraction that differed from the modern strip malls and hustle and bustle of America. The culture of the English pubs, the German gasthaus, or French bakeries fascinated me every day. I enjoyed watching how the locals went about their daily routines and the differences with home. I could find history and culture around every corner.

But more than the history and culture of Europe, it was the people who impressed me. Wherever I went people were helpful, friendly and informative. Throughout Europe people in the cities and the countryside always seemed to have a kind word and would do their best to overcome the language difficulties. Of course, there were a few who were not as charitable or friendly, but those were the exceptions, not the rule. Later, when discussing the summer, I would always say that it was the landscapes of America and the people of Europe that impressed me the most.

August 21 continued:

Thomas and Marianne were both great to me. They are a happy, happy couple – ring or no ring. They are made for each other. They were sure great hosts and have both got good breaks on their jobs. Fantastic schools – better than any I've seen in the U.S. for facilities, equipment, and curriculum. Really like their system. Countryside is rich – its harvest season here. But even in the south where there is good farming the sea and the water are always close and you can see why the Vikings were what they were. The Scandinavians still go down to the sea in an open boat and you can see the square sailed ancestors of the fishing boats and sailors everywhere.

International Economics 101

As I prepared to leave Sweden a new challenge appeared that would bring me great discomfort and uncertainty in the upcoming days. Signs saying, "No U.S. dollar conversion" suddenly appeared at banks and currency exchange booths. I had no idea how it would affect me for the next week.

On Sunday August 15, 1971 President Richard Nixon announced he was taking the United States dollar off the international gold standard in an attempt to control inflation. I did not completely understand what it meant and being in Sweden I did not get any explanation from the local news. It may have been insignificant to the average American back in the States, but it made a huge difference for a traveler in a foreign nation. Due to Nixon's action and the uncertainty of the financial markets, I could not convert U.S. money for local currency. Banks throughout Europe refused to exchange U.S. dollars for the next four or five days while the international exchange rates fluctuated madly and financial institutions tried to figure out the ramifications of Nixon's new policy. I only had a few Swedish kroner, about twenty dollars in U.S. currency, and a couple hundred in travelers' checks. But I could not exchange any of the American money, so I was essentially broke. I was angry, frustrated, and confused. I did not know what to do. I had deliberately chosen to not spend much money on the trip, but I always had the fallback option of cashing a travelers' check if needed. Now that option was gone and I felt helpless.

Many personal issues were created with Nixon's move. I thought the currency exchange problems would be solved in a couple of days, so at first I did not worry too much about it. I did not know it would take almost a week before the financial world would get back to normal. If I had not been with friends it would have been even worse. Thomas loaned me some Swedish kroner, which were still negotiable, but he did not have much money himself, so I spent the next few days with only a few dollars' worth of currency in my pocket.

Normally I was not interested in economics and international finances. At any other time in my life, I would not have paid much attention to this decision. But suddenly my President's political and economic move seemed personally directed at me. I had not been a Nixon fan before, but this financial move seemed personal. In my opinion, he had deliberately waited until I was in Europe to take this action. He knew it would screw up my trip - I was sure of that. Suddenly Nixon was the worst President ever - solely because he maneuvered the economic market to help out the economy of the United States. Looking back, it probably was a good economic decision, but I would never be convinced of that because he made my life miserable for a couple of days. Funny how politics takes on a whole different perspective when it affects you personally.

The next day Thomas and Marianne took me to the coast and bid me farewell as I continued on my journey. I boarded a ferry, then a train to Copenhagen, Denmark. The rest of the trip, I was on my own. The days of staying with friends, sleeping in their homes and eating with them were finished. I was back on the road - this time in another country. It was time to learn about independence and self-determination. Whatever happened would be up to me and the choices I made.

Journal from August 21 continued:

Financially I was hurting in Sweden. With Nixon's ideas for the economy they stopped changing money – so I was stuck w/only about .60 in Swedish Krone. Thank goodness I was w/Thomas. Thank God for Thomas!

Copenhagen

Even though I only spent one day there, I enjoyed Copenhagen. It was the first European city where I was on my own, and I felt an adrenaline rush as I explored the canals and streets of the Danish capital. I found a clean, vibrant, and friendly city.

Of course Copenhagen was famous for its liberal approach to sex and I delighted in some of the openness and freedoms I saw. The ultimate vision of Danish sexual acceptance came while sitting at a sidewalk café having a sandwich and beer. While enjoying the warm summer weather I noticed two young ladies sitting at an outdoor café across the street. It wasn't their good looks that caught my attention – there were plenty of good looking women throughout the city – it was that they were sitting at the café table topless. Not only that, but the more buxom of the two was sitting on the lap of the other, had her arm around her friend's neck and was bouncing up and down, making her breasts bounce high enough to hit her in the chin. The view was erotic, amusing, and entertaining all at the same time. The women were laughing, kissing, and carrying on, while the Danes calmly walked by as if nothing was happening.

That night I stayed at a rather expensive hostel, had a good dinner, and spent money and time at Tivoli Gardens, which was a huge amusement park in the middle of the city and a popular gathering spot for the youth of Copenhagen. I had a couple of beers, watched a lot of beautiful people enjoying a fine summer evening, and found my way back to the youth hostel.

The next day, Sunday, I woke to realize I had spent most of the money Thomas had given me. I had assumed the currency exchange problem would be solved by then, but it wasn't. On the train to Germany I counted my cash and realized the dilemma. I only had about $2.50 worth of Swedish kroner and could not exchange any American traveler's checks. Copenhagen had been fun and exciting, but I had to be more careful with my spending. For the next twenty-four hours, I would have no money for food or travel, but the lesson had been learned.

Journal from August 21 continued:

Aug 16 went on to Denmark. To Copenhagen and H.C. Anderson and the Little Mermaid and beauty. Copenhagen is a beautiful, fantastic city – but cities were made for crowds and especially made for couples. The country is the place of one – the country is the place for me.

Cities are beautiful, but they lose some of their beauty when you're alone.

The Danes, naturally, are much like the Swedes. Very friendly, very helpful and nice. So while Sweden is the land of beautiful people – Denmark is the land of friendliness.

Now I'm on my way to Germany. I spent a lot of money in Denmark (and still missed the first train!) and am going to have to count my Marks from here on. Germany is the land will make – or break – this trip I feel. It could be very exciting and worthwhile and I'm looking forward to seeing very much – but if I run out of time and don't gain anything from it, it could hurt. Of course there is only one reason why I shouldn't gain anything and that is if I don't try to learn anything. The only way this trip can be a failure is if I let it be!

So let's get this damn train movin'. My feet are sore, but it's only the beginning and I've got a lot to see and a lot to learn in this world of ours!

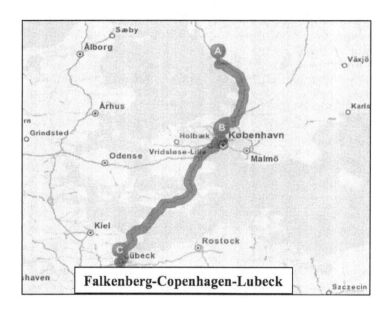

Falkenberg-Copenhagen-Lubeck

On to Germany

The train from Copenhagen to Lubeck, West Germany, only took a couple hours, so I arrived with plenty of time to look around. I discovered an old, historic city with a well preserved medieval center and an interesting place to start learning German history.

In the fourteenth and fifteenth centuries Lubeck was one of the richest trading cities in Northern Europe. As the center of the powerful Hanseatic League, Lubeck dominated trade throughout the Baltic Sea area and north central Europe. As a result the modern city still retained many of its historic buildings, with a unique brick cathedral, one of the oldest hospitals in Europe, and the city's signature icon, the Holstentor - the Hanseatic Gates, which were the old entrance to the city. I enjoyed a quiet afternoon walking through the old city and seeing its medieval architecture.

I still had not been able to exchange any currency, but it was Sunday and very few stores were open. Most of the historic buildings were free to enter, so I concentrated on visiting those. As the day progressed I worried less about my financial situation since I believed the banks would allow currency exchange the next morning. In the meantime I had just enough German Deutsch Marks to buy a candy bar and a Coke. That was my meal for the day.

In the evening I was unsure where to stay and sleep. I found a campground outside of town, but did not have enough money to pay for a campsite. As I was walking through the campground trying to decide what to do, I met an American military family who were stationed in Germany and on vacation in Lubeck. I started talking with them, explained I was in ROTC and would like to be stationed in Germany. That opened a whole line of conversation. The husband was an army colonel who had been in the army for over twenty years. He would be the only active duty military person I would meet on the entire trip through Europe, which was surprising since there were over 50,000 American servicemen stationed in Germany. He was full of recommendations about my future in the army, and was curious about American colleges and the current atmosphere on campus towards the military. He had been out of the States for five or six years, stationed overseas, and his daughter, who was with them, was a junior in high school. The parents were concerned where she should go to college, what type of reception a military brat would get, and if the media reports of riots and demonstrations on campus were true. I did my best to reassure them their daughter would get a good education, and asked them about life in the military. They fed me a hamburger and some chips and made me glad to have met Americans in my time of need. The family's togetherness and kindness impressed me as I left their campsite.

When we first met, I told the military family a small lie. I did not want to admit I did not have a place to stay. I was too proud to admit I was short of cash, so I pretended to have an approved campsite. It was after dark when I left the couple, so I walked to the edge of the campground and found a quiet place behind some trees to rest undetected. That night I did not sleep very well, fearing I might be discovered any minute. Then, at the crack of dawn, I quickly gathered up my bag and snuck out of the campground. I felt guilty not paying, but I was a little desperate, out of money, and figured I did not stay in a full campsite anyway. I made my way to the autobahn and started hitchhiking south.

I had not hitchhiked in Europe yet, having traveled by trains or with friends, but it was time to try my luck with European drivers. There were a number of factors involved in my decision. First, I did not have enough money to buy a train ticket and I had always planned on hitching through Germany. I had heard from fellow travelers the Germans were pretty accepting of hitch-hiking, and it would give me a chance to see if my college German was any good. I did not expect things to be much different from hitchhiking in the States. I knew the German autobahn system was as extensive as the American interstate system and, like back home, as long as you stayed on the entrance ramp the police would not bother you.

Everything I had heard proved to be true. When I got to the autobahn entrance ramp, I found three or four other hitchhikers there and the system of lining up and waiting for rides was the same. It did not take long before a car stopped and picked up another hiker and myself and headed south to Hannover.

Later that day the currency exchange offices opened and my financial problems were solved. I still traveled as cheaply as possible, but at least I had the reassurance I could cash a traveler's check if I needed to.

August 22 – Lubeck, Germany:

Lubeck – what a beautiful town to start a tour of Germany. Really a great place and I hate to go – but it's Sunday and naturally I'm out of money! Flat broke! So I'm on the road again (with 8 other hitchhikers!) I'll say more about Lubeck later.

On August 23 I wrote a postcard to Jackie:

Hi Kiddo - Thought I'd forgotten ya? I didn't! Have had great fun. Have been to Edinburgh, Norway, Sweden (w/ Thomas for 4 days) Copenhagen then down to Germany. Was in Lubeck for one day & that was not enuf. Such a fantastic town. Very old - on an island w/ walls all around & beautiful beautiful churches that truely [sic] reach to God! Saw everything here [on the postcard] and still had time to see more - and I wanted to see more. The old houses here are amazing! Things 500 & 600 yrs. old and people have them spotless! Our mothers would have a riot looking for 14th cent. antiques! Only problem was that it was Sun. & all the stores were closed & there weren't many people around. Plus, I only had about 50 pfennig (15c) and nowhere to cash a travelers check. So I hitchhiked a ride to Hannover in the afternoon and slept in a garage to get outa the rain. Drivers were great & my Deutsch is helping. Today I got a great ride w/a Lutheran pastor who will show me Koln & Bonn tonight & let me sleep in his house. Then on down the Rhein. Everything is going good - hope it keeps up for 10 more days. Not much time, but... Learning much, loving much, and wanting more. See you 9/1

Love Tom

Letters Home

I did not make any journal entries again until September second, when I was on my way home. The last two weeks of my trip went by fast and I was always on the move with no place or opportunity to put my thoughts on paper. However, I did write a couple of letters and postcards home that summarized the events and my impressions of the trip. Over the course of the European portion of the summer I realized how much I was out of contact with my loved ones. I had made two long distance telephone calls home - "Collect for Tom Laughlin" - one from London and one from Sweden when I got to Thomas'. Otherwise, my parents had little idea where I was or what I was doing. So when I did have a chance to write, I wrote my parents and Jackie instead of taking the time for journal entries. Since I wrote so rarely, those letters were crammed full of information. They contained the same type of commentary as the journal entries and my parents kept them. On August twenty-third, I wrote about my journey from Lubeck to Cologne, Germany. The letter did not follow my trip chronologically, but did comment on some very significant events of the summer.

August 23
German Autobahn
(on the way to Koln and Bonn)

Dear Home,

Well, I was in Hanover last night. Looked all over for Bama but I couldn't find her. She was probably out tricycling or partying! Luckily she left her garage open – so I slept there. Excuse me if this gets too sloppy, I'm in a VW Bus going 120 Km/hr.

My maternal grandmother, whose nickname was Bama, lived in Hanover, Michigan. That was where my mother grew up, so the comment about Bama and Hanover was meant as a family joke. I had an interesting night in Hannover, Germany though. I saw very little of the city, since I was dropped off from my last ride late in the evening. The driver took me to a huge park in the center of town and pointed out the direction of the youth hostel. However, the hostel was full, so I decided to go back to the park and find a sleeping spot. The park was full of young people and seemed to be a popular hangout. Groups were talking, playing music, smoking a little weed, and having a nice evening together. I met a couple of young Germans who spoke English and they filled me in on the local park culture and rules about sleeping in the park.

Just as we were discussing sleeping in the park, a violent thunderstorm came up and threatened to soak us. In desperation to get out of the storm, the three of us ducked into the open garage of a nearby home. After standing there for about an hour with no letup to the storm in sight, we decided to stay put and sleep on the concrete floor of the garage as best we could. I remember thinking it seemed a little strange, and very trustworthy, of the homeowner to leave his garage door open all night, but I was thankful he did, since I was able to stay dry. My curiosity was answered at 5:00 AM the next morning when the owner came to the door of the garage and very nicely said, "Alright boys, the storm has past. It's time for you to go now." I realized he knew we were there all night and had let us stay to get out of the storm. This was one more example of the trust and openness I experienced throughout my travels.

Letter of August 23 continued:

Have been hitching since Lubeck (yesterday) and have had some of the most rewarding educational rides I've ever had. Three guys w/varying degrees of broken English and me w/my terrible degree of broken German. One thing that has been great is how well we communicate. Also, my last 2 rides have been Lutheran pastors who have been very verbal and talked a lot about German life and were very helpful to me. Mein bissen Deutsch has been quite helpful. (Coming into the Ruhr Valley and I'd like to look around – so more later.)...

Lubeck was a great city, It was a perfect place to start my trip to Germany. Beautifully built churches w/steeples that touched the sky. And old winding streets w/lots of history and lots of Germany in them. I just walked the streets for 6 hours w/my mouth open and loving it all. I would have liked to have been there longer, but...#1 – It was Sun. and all the shops were closed. #2 – I only had ½ Mark (15 cents) to my name and no where to cash a check. And #3 – time is becoming very precious.

Went to Lubeck from Copenhagen by train (notice you get things backwards? – Sorry) Nice little ride through Denmark. Copenhagen was very, very nice. It is a very friendly city and lots of fun. Hans Christian Anderson is all over and I wanted to buy you a book of his fairy tales Mom, but I blew it (explained later). However, I did manage to buy myself a hand knit Scandinavian turtle-neck sweater. I think it's nice.

Took a train from Falkenberg to Copenhagen. Passed by Elsinore (Hamlet's Castle) Looked like a very nice place but the conductor wouldn't let me off.

That takes me back to Thomas. He was so good to me. I thoroughly enjoyed myself doing nothing but relaxing and talking to Thomas and Marianne. She is a fantastic girl and has eyes that would send any boy on a trip – including Thomas. They get along beautifully and work together so much it's great. They truly are a good couple. Their apt. is very nice – very modern and they are getting new furniture for it. Their schools are unreal and are better equipped, I think, than any I've ever seen in the states! All in all, I have nothing but good things to say about those two. They were too good to me.

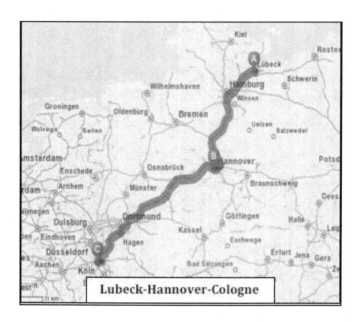

Lubeck-Hannover-Cologne

My German Saint

A few years ago there was an expression going around of "What would Jesus do?" and people wore bracelets with the letters WWJD to remind them of what to do in various circumstances. Personally, if I were to wear something like that, it would have to say WWHWD – for "What would Herr Winckler do?" This gentleman was a saint. My letter home only scratches the surface of what he did for others. Fredrick Winckler was a Lutheran minister who would become my shining example of kindness and caring over the next twenty-four hours.

Herr Winckler picked me up in an old Volkswagen van on the entrance to the autobahn outside Hannover. He was in his late thirties, about six feet tall with a barrel chest, a round smiling face, and a receding hairline. He was gregarious, quietly self-assured, and the most trusting man I have ever met. He was comfortable in his own skin. I had taken German for two years in college, but was far from fluent. None the less, with his broken English, and my smattering of German, we were able to communicate quite well. After the usual small talk and getting acquainted - where I was from, what I was doing, where I was going, etc. - he explained he was going to Cologne and I was welcome to go with him. I quickly agreed, since the great cathedral of Cologne was something I wanted to see. He mentioned he had to stop at a small village church for about an hour and if I cared to wait for him, he would then take me on to Cologne. Since I could spend over an hour waiting at the autobahn for the next ride, I told him I would be glad to wait. I would walk around the village while waiting.

When we stopped at the church where his meeting was held, his inherent trust in people became obvious. As I got out of the van he turned to me and said, "Here, you take my keys."

I looked at him with a quizzical look on my face and he said, "You will probably return to the van before I am done. If so, you may want to get in and rest."

"I can just wait on the steps," I protested.

"Think nothing of it. I trust you," And he went inside.

As he walked away the implications of what he had done started to hit me. He had known me for less than an hour and yet trusted me enough to give me the keys to his van. I was amazed as I watched him go into the church. I started realizing this was a very special gentleman.

His honesty and openness continued as we traveled down the autobahn toward Cologne. He mentioned he had been born just before World War II and had lived in Cologne. At my suggestion, he started recalling what he remembered of the bombing of Cologne. Even though he was only about three or four years old, the vividness of his recall made it clear how emotionally upsetting the experience had been for him.

"Before the war my family lived in the old town center. It was a close knit area with houses right on top of each other. Even though I was small I can still remember the narrow streets, the smells, and the neighborhood. It was a typical medieval city. In the center of it all was the cathedral."

He hesitated as he drove down the autobahn, thinking back to those violent experiences of his youth.

"In 1942, when I was about four, the Allies started bombing Cologne. We would go to our bomb-shelters and wait it out, but usually they were bombing the industrial areas on the outskirts of town. But one night they bombed the center of town. It was right over my head and seemed like it went on forever. My most vivid memory was coming out of the shelter the next morning. The entire neighborhood was gone and there was fire all around us. But in the middle of all that destruction, the cathedral still stood intact. Der Dom - the cathedral - became our sign of hope and renewal during the war.

"After that my mother took me to a relative's in the country until the end of the war. I will never forget the destruction and horror of that day though. It is what led me to become a minister - to try to stop wars and hatred among people. It is true what they say - war is Hell."

As he described these events he looked off into the distance with a painful look in his eyes. His personal experiences became my experiences. I remember the look on his face as he was transported back to the war by his memories of the terror and destruction. Yet, this man, who had personally experienced the most destructive, hate-filled, life changing war of all time, was kind, trusting, and full of faith in the goodness of people.

It was mid-afternoon as we approached Cologne.

"Do you have friends in the city? Where will you be staying tonight?" asked Herr Winckler.

"You can just take me into the city. I'll look around a little and find a youth hostel to stay in," I said.

"First you must stop at my house and meet my wife. We can have a little afternoon snack and then I will take you into the city and show you around."

Soon we were at the old, character filled, half-timbered home of the Wincklers. When he introduced me to his wife she greeted me with the same warmth and kindness I had received from him. Although she had no idea I was coming, she gave me a warm welcome and prepared an afternoon snack, all the while asking many questions about my trip, my family, and what I would want for dinner. She brought out a tray of delicious cheese, crackers, and sliced meats. It was more food than I had seen in many days. While she was preparing the snack Herr Winckler went to the cellar and brought out a fine bottle of wine. As I sat in their living room I felt like a long lost friend instead of a young American whom they had just met.

My family had always been interested in antiques, so I took note of the Winckler's beautiful family antiques. There were two grandfather clocks older than the United States, an ancient family hutch, and a six inch thick Bible sitting on the coffee table with all the births and deaths of the family recorded going back to the 1700s. Additionally, the house had been in the family for over three hundred years. Despite the home's age, the interior was modern and extremely comfortable.

Frau Winckler cared for me like a mother and asked, "Where will you be staying tonight?" When I explained my usual eating and sleeping arrangements to her, she said. "Of course you will do no such thing. I insist you stay here. We have a spare bedroom where you can wash up, have dinner with us, and get a good night's rest. I insist." Herr Winckler just smiled and nodded his head in agreement.

How could I refuse? I took my first shower in three days and changed clothes, and then Herr Winckler and I headed into Cologne for his personalized tour. While I was gone, Frau Winckler insisted on washing my clothes - which again I found impossible to refuse. Herr Winckler took me to the Cologne Cathedral and explained the history of the massive cathedral, gothic architecture, and the surrounding neighborhood. Having lived in its shadow most of his life, he was able to talk about his personal experiences at this historic site. It was much more informative - and personal - than I could have ever experienced on my own.

After walking through the old city center of Cologne, we drove to Bonn, which at that time was West Germany's capitol. While I enjoyed seeing the cities, I saw even more examples of the kindness of my host. Twice on the trip, to and from Bonn, Herr Winckler stopped to help stranded motorists whose cars had broken down - even towing one couple's car about five miles to a service station late in the evening. I realized the kindness the Wincklers had shown me was nothing special for them – it was how they chose to live their lives.

That night I slept in an extremely comfortable feather bed. As I reflected on the events of the day I realized I was a very lucky young man.

The next morning I was served a huge, delicious breakfast of fresh pastries, cheeses, and hard boiled eggs. Then, Herr Winckler explained he would help me get a ride south towards Frankfurt – my next destination. As I prepared to leave, his wife handed me a large paper bag, explaining she had packed a lunch for the trip. Later I discovered two large sandwiches, some cheese, and three pieces of fruit. It was more food than I had eaten for much of the trip. Frau Winckler's lunch bag provided food for my next three days.

Herr Winckler drove me to an autobahn rest-stop, looked around for a nice looking gentleman and proceeded to ask the driver if he would be willing to take me south to the Frankfurt/Heidelberg area. Without having to do anything, he had me speeding down the autobahn on my way to Heidelberg. Although I later sent flowers to the Wincklers as a small token of my appreciation, I'm sure they had no idea how much impact they had on my life. I sent them Christmas cards for a few years, and eventually lost touch with them. But the memory of what they did will always be with me.

As I look back on my experience with the Wincklers, I appreciate the kindness and faith they demonstrated. If holiness involves living your life in the example of Christ and his teachings, then this was the most holy couple I have ever met. All religions teach we should be kind to our fellow man, but this couple lived that life to the ultimate. Herr Winckler and his wife met me when I was down and out, took care of me, revitalized me, and sent me on my way with a new spirit and a new outlook on humanity. For that they will never be forgotten.

Growing up, my mother would read Henry Van Dyke's short story "The Other Wiseman" to me at Christmas time. When thinking of the Wincklers I always think of the climactic line of that story: As Artaban, the main character, lies dying, he hears the Lord's voice and asks,

Not so, my Lord! For when saw I thee hungered and fed thee? Or thirsty, and gave thee drink? When saw I thee a stranger, and took thee in? Or naked, and clothed thee? When saw I thee sick or in prison, and came unto thee."...

"And a voice seemed to say, "Verily I say unto thee, Inasmuch as thou hast done it unto one of the least of these my brethren, thou hast done it unto me.

Letter home on August 23 (continued):

Am settled now – and you'll never believe where – in a home of my last driver. He is a Lutheran pastor and lives near Koln (Cologne). He is going to take me into the Cologne Cathedral (Der Dom) and the city of Bonn (capital of W. Germany) tonight and then let me stay here tonight. Tomorrow he will take me to the Autobahn and show me the way to Frankfurt and Worms and the Rhine Valley. A beautiful home and beautiful man w/ a beautiful family. All I can think of is the Bible passage – which I must destroy since I don't know the Bible well – "I was tired and hungry and low in spirit and you took me in and gave me food and drink and rest..." (I think it goes like that – I think you know what I mean.)

The Summer of '71

This is a very nice home w/unbelievable furniture. Mom – I had tea from china that looked about 100 years old – in a room w/a chest from 1591, and china cabinet 300 yrs. old w/200-250 yr old tin & silver & clay coffee pots and dishes in it – under an operating, chiming, fantastic clock from 1805 on a 100-150 yr old table! Then I went down stairs to shower (yeah – shower!) and there was a 7' high, operating Grandfather clock w/a beautiful finish and hand carving w/a date 1712 on the face. Oh – I forgot to mention the Bibles sitting on the chest – one in old Germany from 1719 – it's the family Bible w/birthdays and things written in it – and another huge Bible dating from 1666! W/copper plate pictures in it yet! The entire room was priceless – amazing! Ages over here are something else. I don't mean this as a slam Mom, but your oldest antique would just barely deserve the name "antique" over here. People live in houses 4-5 hundred yrs old and the thing is spotless! In Lubeck there were houses from the Middle Ages and families were scrubbing, painting, repairing them just as if they were only 2 days old.

But Fredrich Winckler (good German name) is treating me like royalty. He is such a very very GOOD man – from deep in his heart – he is good all thru – and so helpful and trustworthy. Und seine Frau also. [an attempt to say "and his wife too!] He took me to Cologne and Bonn – the cathedral is so gorgeous it is beyond belief. That Middle Age man could work for 500 years to build it – it is a monument to their lives, and as Herr Winckler said, "They did it entirely for God!" About all I can say about Bonn is that I've seen the German capital and Beethoven's home – but it wasn't too much. But tomorrow, I'm on down the Rhine & then to France, Amsterdam & home. See you then. (which is Sept. 1st).

A German History Lesson

Herr Winckler set me up with a comfortable ride in a Mercedes, but my driver did not speak English, and my broken German made conversation limited, so it was a quiet trip south. After only a couple of hours of comfortably speeding down the German autobahn, we arrived in Heidelberg. Around noon my driver dropped me off near the center of town and I proceeded to take in some of the more historic parts of Germany.

During the next twenty-four hours I would visit Heidelberg, Speyer, and Worms. It was a very condensed German history lesson. Although I was a history major, and a devoted history lover, most of my studies had been in American history. My only class in European history had been a general Western Civilization course as a freshman. That class skimmed the surface of European history and did not mention most of the places visited on my trip except London and Paris. But after Heidelberg, Speyer, and Worms, I became determined to study the history of Germany and central Europe in much greater depth. All three towns were steeped in history, and after visiting them, I wanted to know more.

Heidelberg was a beautiful town located along the Neckar River and dominated by the medieval prince's castle half way up the mountain. Its narrow streets, half-timbered houses, and culture exuded German style. It was a romantic, classic, setting which made it easy to love. It also was an academic center, being the home of the oldest university in Germany. Consequently, it was a popular gathering spot for many youth, both German and American tourists alike.

The town square was filled with college age students, many of whom were American students spending a European summer similar to mine. It was easy to join the conversations of these fellow travelers. Some had similar experiences of staying in hostels, sleeping in train stations, traveling with little money, and having little to eat. Others were on expensive, all-inclusive tours and marveling at the hippies (which seemed to be the catch-all phrase for anyone traveling by themselves.) just hanging out in the town square. But I did not meet anyone with experiences like mine of close friends, benevolent pastors, friendly rail conductors, or drivers who took them out of their way. And no one had hitchhiked across the United States and Europe all in one summer.

The youth culture in Heidelberg demonstrated the difference between the communism of Eastern Europe, and the freedom of the West. What best illustrated that difference was the black market value of American blue jeans. American students were selling blue jeans brought from the states to buyers who would sell them on the black market in Eastern Europe. Jeans that could be bought for $15 - $20 in the States were being sold for over $100 - and it did not seem to matter what condition they were in. One couple who needed money sold the dirty, holey jeans they had on, then went to a nearby store - in their undershorts - and bought a pair of cheap German sweat pants. This brought me to my conclusion that communism fell because of exposure to western fashion and culture.

I enjoyed the castle and history of Heidelberg, but it was too touristy and there were too many college kids. The city was packed with kids talking, trying to beg money from others, and generally looking pathetic. I wanted to get away for a quiet evening, so I took a bus ride about twenty miles to the town of Speyer. I arrived late in the evening, but was greeted by the immense Romanesque cathedral that dominated the town. It had been a long day, it was late, and I was hungry, so I made it a point to visit the cathedral the next day.

Speyer did not have a youth hostel or a campground available that late at night. The local hotels were too expensive for an eight hour stay. I was told there was a park about two miles out of town, but it seemed too far away. Finally, about 11:00 at night, exhausted and frustrated from not finding a better sleeping spot, I noticed a quiet spot next to an abandoned railroad line. I looked around, saw no lights or sign of regular usage of the tracks, and decided that would be my bed for the night. I gathered up some leaves and grass to make a cushion, spread out my sleeping bag, and quickly went to sleep. As I settled in to my make-shift nest for the night, I wondered what Mom would think if she knew where I was sleeping. I figured it was best she did not know. Sleeping next to the railroad tracks seems desperate today, but at the time it proved quite comfortable and restful. I did not want to spend another restless night sitting up in a rail station and did not want to spend the money for the local hotels, so it seemed like the best alternative. I must not have been concerned about a train coming, robbery, or anything else, because I slept very well.

Speyer cathedral had been the coronation site for the Emperor of the Holy Roman Empire from the 11th century until the early 19th century when the Empire ceased to exist. The cathedral - Der Kaisardom - was a spectacular example of German Romanesque architecture, which was characterized by thick, heavy walls, and rounded arches to bear the weight of the immense building. Der Kaisardom was over 400 feet long and 100 feet high. The cathedral in Cologne was larger, but the gothic style in Cologne - the pointed arches, larger windows, and lighter, thinner walls - made Cologne seem smaller and more personal. The heavy, thick walls and small windows of Speyer gave it a powerful, foreboding feel which seemed appropriate for a church so closely tied to the Holy Roman Emperor. Speyer was a small town and this great architectural wonder, in the middle of town, fascinated me. I had read about medieval cathedrals in college and now I could study one of the largest and most famous. I spent over two hours studying the cathedral, visiting its museum, and admiring its beauty.

Next stop was the city of Worms. Like Heidelberg and Speyer, Worms was another very old, medieval town with an extensive historical tradition. And, like Speyer, it had a spectacular Romanesque cathedral that captivated most of my attention. Worms considered itself the birthplace of the Protestant Reformation. It was there that Martin Luther made his stand against the demands of the Holy Roman Emperor and refused to renounce his teachings. Fascinated by this history, I spent most of the day wandering through the cathedral and associated museums. By the end of the day I was tired and proceeded by train further north to Mainz.

Mainz also had a strong historical significance – with another large cathedral and the home of Gutenberg's first printing press – but I had seen enough history for one day. The train arrived in Mainz at 7:00 p.m., so it was too late to visit anything. I was tired and not that interested in Mainz, so I decided to take the night train to Paris. Many of the youth in Heidelberg had exclaimed how the French did not like American hitchhikers. There were stories of hitchhikers being run off the road, dropped off in strange places, or just ignored in France, so I made up my mind not to tempt fate - I would take the train to Paris. The night train provided a place to sleep during the trip and I would arrive in Paris the next morning. It had been a fast, but rewarding trip through Germany. I had only spent $200 so far in Europe, so I was feeling good.

I wrote another letter on August twenty-fifth about my adventures in Germany.

Aug. 25, Mainz, Germany

Dear Home,

Well, I'm waiting for my train to Paris so I thought I'd write again. Can't figure out what's getting into me – writing all these letters and all. Maybe a lot has happened in 2 days? Maybe I didn't say everything in my last one? Maybe I'm getting just a teeny-weeny bit homesick? Maybe I'm dead tired and need something to do so I don't fall asleep and miss my train?... Maybe it's a combination of those and a few more reasons!

No. 1 – Yeah, a lot has happened in 2 days. Tues. morning Herr Winckler drove me over to an Autobahn service area, walked up to a guy and said (In Deutsch naturally) "Will you take my friend here to Frankfurt w/you?" Only a little more elaborately. The guy said "sure" and I was on my way. Of course that was after a good German breakfast (bread & butter, bread & marmalade, bread & cheese, and tea!) then Frau Winckler packed me a lunch! Well, I rode with this guy past Frankfurt to Heidelberg. I didn't quite "Lose my Heart in Heidelberg." Heidelberg is very nice and romantic like and all – really pretty. From there I went to a little town on the Rhine called Speyer. Got there about 9:00 PM, so, after walking around for a while, I found a nice grassy spot next to an old abandoned railroad track and collapsed. Slept well – really! This morning I walked around Speyer – was fun 'cuz I was bout the only tourist and they have a fantastic 11th c. cathedral, plus a lot of old narrow streets. From there I took a train to Worms (which is another one of my wonderful "how-to-miss-a-train-almost-but-not-quite-miss-it-cuz-you-can't-tell-time" stories). Worms is the town where Martin Luther made his stand against the Emperor. More churches, more narrow streets, and by now you can see I'm getting tired of telling you about beautiful cathedrals and narrow streets. So I went on to Mainz. By now I have gone down one side of the Rhine and up the other (or is it up one side and down the other?) I got to Mainz about 7:00 PM which was too late to see anything, So I talked myself into going to Paris tonight. (I'm getting a little tired of beautiful cathedrals, etc. myself!) Of course I had until 11:00 so three hours of seeing Mainz by night. It's OK, but NYC has a better night life. Sooo – here I is! Would like to see the German and French countryside 'tween here and Paris, but I guess I won't. Will be in Paris about 7:10 AM tomorrow.

If this sounds depressing or something like that – don't worry, I'm not really down. It's mainly that I've caught myself in the "See Europe in ten days" syndrome and I catch myself saying "hurry, hurry – can't see this museum or street 'cuz I got to get to ___ where I can see that beautiful cathedral..." That's what I did yesterday and today anyways. And I hate myself for it! That's why I'm going to Paris now – Hopefully I'll be able to relax there more.

Guess I am getting a bit homesick – only one week from tomorrow. As far as I can tell we will still be in the

1st – whether at 1AM or 11PM I don't know. Guess about all I can do is call from Metro when I get in – But don't wait around home if you have something else to do – I can call Jackie or many other people who can get me. So do what you want (Maybe Jac will want to come anyways??) But can I ask for a little favor? Like, order a meal – American style! Like steak, potatoes (anykind) FRESH vegetables, FRESH salad, NICE COLD MILK and good American dessert I can put lots of Amer. ice cream on! Maybe a little drinkie-pooh (not beer!) beforehand? And maybe whatever else my loving Mother can dream up! Well – there goes my dream of the night! See how this one turns out!

Guess that's about it. Sent the Wincklers some flowers and my German was so good I naturally paid more than I wanted to – or should have. But money is ok! Just went over the $200 mark w/ the $20 I needed to go to Paris and $30 of what I don't count. So I've told myself I'm coming home with $200 – maybe more! It's the Scotch in me! Well good night for now – have to go count my pfennig.

All my Love
Tom

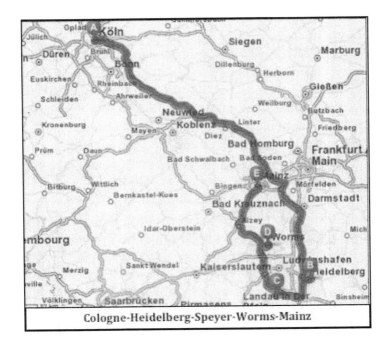

Cologne-Heidelberg-Speyer-Worms-Mainz

Paris - Alone in a Big Crowd

On the way to Paris my good luck making new friends continued. Across the aisle on the train were a young American college study abroad student and his French girlfriend. It did not take long before we started a conversation and struck up a casual friendship. The young woman was house sitting a flat in Paris for her aunt, and by the time we reached Paris the next morning they had invited me to stay with them that evening. So, with the address in my pocket, I set out to see the City of Lights.

I am sure if I had called home and told my mother I was in Paris, she would have been very excited and would have expected it to be the highlight of the trip, but unfortunately it became a depressing low point. The first two weeks of the trip were a time of companionship and help from Mick, Brian, and Thomas. But I had been alone traveling through Denmark and Germany. While the freedom and independence were enlightening and were one of the reasons I had chosen to travel solo and not take a tour, I was starting to feel stressed and lonely. I had been traveling by myself for most of three months. The excitement of hitchhiking, being on my own, and adjusting to changing circumstances was starting to get old.

The inability to make phone calls, get mail, or make any significant contact with loved ones at home was starting to make me homesick. This is another example of how the communications revolution has changed things. If I were making the same trip today I would be able to email or call home easily. But that was not the case in 1971. Although I did not call or write often while in the States, at least the opportunity was there and I could call if needed. In Europe, I did not have that crutch to fall back on and the more I was on my own, the more I realized how important it was to be able to communicate with loved ones. While isolation was part of the challenge of the summer experience, it still hit me hard. I had to remember I would be back amongst friends and family in a little over a week. There were still places in Europe I wanted to see and things I wanted to do, but more and more I had thoughts of home.

Paris seemed to exacerbate the feeling of helplessness and homesickness. I had been by myself in big cities before – London in particular – but had always found other Americans to explore with, talk to, and laugh with. Throughout the European portion of the summer there had been very few days when I had not been able to share ideas and impressions with other Americans. But Paris became the loneliest city of the summer. My house sitting friends had seen plenty of Paris, so they were not traveling around, and throughout the day I did not meet any other American students. The language barrier made everything more complicated and frustrating. In Scandinavia and Germany I had been able to communicate with the local population, which was one of the most enjoyable parts of those experiences. But, I did not speak French, and that developed into a problem. Many French did not speak English and it seemed they did not want to try to communicate with anyone who could not speak their language. Consequently, I found myself trying to get around with very little local assistance.

My day in Paris consisted of seeing most of the standard tourist sites quickly and efficiently. Notre Dame, the Louvre, the Champs de Elysees, the Arch of Triumph, and the Eifel Tower consumed most of the day. It was enjoyable to walk the streets and see the sights of central Paris. While each visit was as short as possible, I still was able to experience much of the central city.

Again, the grandeur and architecture at the Cathedral of Notre Dame got most of my attention. While the cathedrals at Speyer and Worms were massive and awesome due to their size, the light and airy gothic architecture of Notre Dame quickly made it a favorite. The first steps into the tall, stately sanctuary took my breath away and I found myself irresistibly drawn to the heights of the ceiling and looking up to God - just as the medieval architects had intended. The brilliant colors coming through the stained glass window gave a pinkish tint to everything. I paused, sat down, and thought of the marvelous ingenuity of medieval society. It was hard to comprehend medieval workers patiently taking over 200 years to build this masterpiece, yet the result of their handicraft was all around me.

The gargoyles of Notre Dame overlooking Paris.

I took some time and reflected on the unforgettable experiences of my summer. I had found the love of God in the stark, harsh beauty of a Wyoming sunrise and in the kindness of a myriad of wonderful people who picked me up and took me down the road. I had been helped through difficult situations in unfamiliar places by saintly strangers, and had visited some of the cultural wonders of history. And now, near the end of my journey, I was in one of the most beautiful manmade structures dedicated to the power of God. I could not forget my parents and the love and faith they had to allow me, and even encourage me, to have this experience. I could not help but realize how blessed I had been throughout the summer. God had watched over me and shown me the love of the world and humanity in a short period of time. I would not forget that.

The rest of the day was a blur. I could not spend much time in the Louvre, but I wanted to see the *Mona Lisa*. It took two hours to get through the lines to see her, and at first glance I was disappointed. Mona was not as big, or as dramatic, as expected, but after reflecting on da Vinci's masterpiece I saw the beautiful simplicity of the work and the mystical character of Mona Lisa's face.

It was a warm summer afternoon when I left the Louvre to leisurely walk the mile up the Champs de Elysees to the Arch of Triumph, watching people, looking at the high prices, and making a vow to someday return to shop and relax at an outdoor cafe. In the meantime, I saved my francs and enjoyed the scenery and people.

After climbing the Eifel Tower, and enjoying the view of Paris, I decided it was time to find my Parisian friends. I took the Metro to an outlying suburb and found the address. They had asked three other couples over for the evening and I was invited to join the party. They were all young French college students, who were very friendly, but only spoke broken English, so conversation was limited. The group was very nice and helpful, but I was the outsider. My earlier concerns about being the loner and being a stranger seemed to manifest themselves in this gathering.

Sitting and watching the party gave me an opportunity to reflect and realize how easy it is to be lonely, even in a crowd. The same melancholy mood had come over me in Seattle earlier in the summer. At the beginning of my trip around Europe I had been among friends and could share conversation on many topics, but the last few days I had been by myself. I had made temporary friendships and had talked to many people, but the conversations were usually very much the same and became repetitious and rote. I was getting bored with those conversations. So while I was having a great time and meeting wonderful people, I realized how important it was to have family, loved ones, and close friends to travel and share experiences with. I have continued to travel, but ever since, I have always enjoyed having a companion.

After a couple of glasses of wine, the extensive walking of the day caught up with me and I found a small corner, spread out my sleeping bag, and went to sleep.

The next day we all slept in. It felt good to be lazy and not have to rush somewhere. It was almost noon when I said goodbye to my hosts and went back to the streets of Paris. I had intended on more sightseeing and then to take an evening train to Brussels, Belgium, so I could sleep onboard the train again, but things changed as I rode the Metro to the center of Paris. Without any warning I became sick to my stomach and feverish. I quickly got off at the next stop, hoping some fresh air would help me feel better. I barely made it to the street where I sat down on the curb and puked in the gutter. When I got a chance, I looked up at the people around me. I was dizzy, feverish, could not see straight, and sick to my stomach, but not one Parisian stopped to help or ask how I was. I thought of all the times strangers had helped me on my trip - the neighbors in Sweden offering a cup of coffee, the man who kept his garage open for shelter during the rain storm, and of course the Wincklers - but in Paris I was invisible. I sat on the curb with my head over the gutter and I thought, *What an iconic view of Paris - to be looking down at a street gutter...* I do not know what caused my upset stomach, but it was indicative of the low point of the trip. In about fifteen minutes I recovered enough to continue, but those moments in the gutter became symbolic of my visit to Paris.

I walked around Paris, but I no longer felt like visiting Montmartre or any of the other sites I had on my list. I decided to go to the train station and leave early for Brussels. At the Paris Gare de Nord station my bad luck with the French continued.

When I arrived at the station I took my time to make sure I was reading the schedule correctly. I was pretty sure, with my limited French, that the column marked "arriver" meant when trains were arriving, and the column marked "sortie" was the departure times. So I patiently waited my turn and stepped up to the ticket counter.

"Parlez vous Anglais?" I asked the man behind the counter, hoping he would speak English.

He just shook his head.

"Sprechen sie Deutsch?" I asked, hoping to use my German.

He just glared at me, like I was an idiot.

"Okay then, I want a train to Brussels - au Bruxelles s'il vous plaî..." I asked as nicely as I could, using my hand to point to the timetable next to him and pointing to the word "Bruxelles" at the same time.

Again, the man glared at me, mumbled something that I took for "Stupid American!" then shocked me by sticking the "Closed" sign in the ticket window and walking away. I had heard stories of rude and arrogant Frenchmen, but here he was in the flesh. I was flabbergasted, mad, sick, and feeling like I wanted to hit something or someone.

Just then a gentlemanly Frenchman, who was behind me in line and watching all this, asked in very good English, "May I help you?"

"I just want to get the next train to Brussels," I said. He smiled, stepped up to the same window, flagged down another salesman and bought me a ticket. I could not believe it - in about two minutes time I had met one of the rudest Frenchmen and one of the nicest. I paid for my ticket, thanked my good Samaritan, and went to find my train to Brussels.

Paris had been a disappointing part of the summer, but I made a vow to someday return and experience it in style. I did not know when, but I knew it would happen.

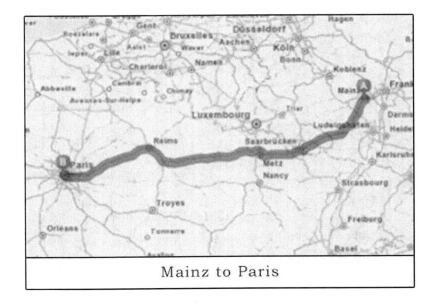

Mainz to Paris

On to the Lowlands

The train to Brussels was direct and I arrived about 9:00 PM. A quick walk around the neighborhood proved it was much too late to find a room, since the hostels and cheap hotels near the station were either full or closed, so I returned to the train station to spend the night there.

I had not experienced any difficulties at the other rail stations I had stayed at, so I was not concerned about this one. But Belgium had a unique rule that made things a little more complicated. If you did not have a ticket for an early morning train, you could not stay in the station. If you did, you could be arrested for vagrancy. I bought the cheapest ticket possible, which was still cheaper than a hotel, and tried to find a quiet spot to sleep. But the Belgians had one more trick to keep people from spending the night in the station. As the custodians cleaned the floors they moved everyone out of the area and they always seemed to be cleaning the spot where I was trying to sleep. Consequently, I was awakened and moved often as the night progressed. I made it through the night, but got very little sleep.

It was Sunday, August twenty-ninth, which meant there were only three days left before my flight home. I wanted to make the most of the time I had left. I did what most tourists do in Brussels, bought a Belgian waffle, then walked around the medieval city center and marveled at the beautiful City Hall. But most of all, I wanted to go to Waterloo.

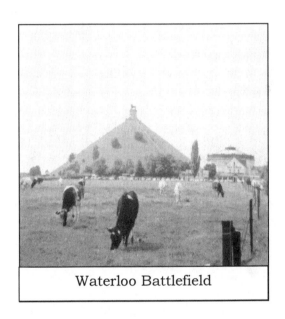

Waterloo Battlefield

We had studied Napoleon in my military history classes so I knew Waterloo was near Brussels. I went to the bus station, bought a ticket and took a forty-five minute ride to the battlefield. I had been to a number of Civil War battlefields in the United States and assumed Waterloo would be as well organized and an enjoyable experience. It would seem one of the most important battles in the history of Europe would have a well preserved battlefield and good documentation of the events - a bit like Gettysburg in the United States. Boy was I mistaken.

My first impression of the battlefield came when I saw a herd of cattle grazing in the fields. I thought, *This can't be one of the greatest battlefields in history, with cows just wandering around!* There were a couple of cannon scattered around and a huge mound of earth with a large statue on top. After climbing several hundred steps, I discovered a statue of a lion and a memorial to the British soldiers who died during the battle. From the top of the mound it was easy to see the whole battlefield, but there was very little description of what happened and how the battle was fought. Today, I understand, there is a much more elaborate tourist site and museum depicting the battle, but in 1971 there was not much to look at. Disappointed and frustrated, I took the bus back to Brussels and found a youth hostel with a bed open. At least I got a decent night's sleep that evening.

The next day I decided to try my luck hitchhiking again. Fellow travelers in the hostel had said it was easy to hitch a ride north to Amsterdam, and I had been very lucky in Germany, so it seemed logical to get back to the road. By early afternoon I was on the highway speeding north into the Netherlands. After a brief delay about fifty miles outside of Amsterdam I got a ride from an older, rather rough looking, Dutchman who said he would take me into the city. Everything seemed to be proceeding fine.

This turned into the only threatening ride of the entire summer. The little Dutchman had a very small car - one of those with only enough room for two seats, a gear shift in between and not much else. He did not speak English, but my broken German was good enough for basic communication. We got through the normal introductions and brief history of where I had been. We had an hour drive to Amsterdam so I daydreamed and conversation lagged until we came to the outskirts of Amsterdam. It was early evening as we approached the city, when my driver casually asked where I would be staying that night. Since there was nothing unusual about that question I said, "I'll find a hostel in Amsterdam."

"You could stay at my place," he stated in German.

"Nein danke" - no thanks, I said. My senses were on alert. There was something about this guy I did not like, even though he had been most accommodating until now.

He then started on a different tact, and asked me if I was an athlete. "Bist du ein Sportman?" he asked.

"Ja, eine bishen" - a little, I replied. "Basketball and American football."

"Ah, das gute! Ein Sportman!" and he reached over and grabbed my left leg on the knee.

When I did not respond, he continued, "Sportman - Ja!" and grabbed my lower thigh a couple inches above my knee. Now I was getting nervous.

"No!" I said emphatically.

"Oh ja! Sportman!" He said again, ignoring my objections. His hand moved higher up my thigh.

I knew it was time to get out of there. I grabbed his hand, pushed it away and made a disapproving face. Then, as we came to a stop light, I grabbed my bag, opened the door, got out, and walked away. I had rehearsed the move many times in my mind over the months on the road, but had never had to use it. Now I was glad I had thought about it in advance. After all those miles, I had met my first - and last - undesirable driver.

After he drove off, I started thinking what might have happened if I had taken him up on the offer to stay at his place. Considering how many overnight stays I had accepted from strangers, it was surprising I did not accept this one. But my intuition told me there was something about the guy. The more I thought about his conversation and actions I knew I had been lucky. I also reflected back to my experience in San Francisco. There, the friendly, polite, calm young man had not been any threat. Here - although I was never directly propositioned by the Dutchman - I felt threatened and was physically shaken. I shuddered with the thought of what might have happened if I had gone with him.

I took the bus in to Amsterdam. I got into town after dark, found a hostel with a bunk open, and settled in. Like any good college student in Amsterdam, I wanted to experience the famous night life of the city. I walked through the famous Red Light District (no I did not stop - way too much money - but of course you can always look can't you?), and stopped at a couple of bars for a quick beer. I was getting bored with the solo nightlife. After a number of nights alone, bars started looking the same anywhere in the world. It was time to return to the hostel for the night.

Amsterdam was the last stop of the summer before heading home. In order to make sure nothing went wrong, the first thing I did the next morning was go to the railroad station and buy my ticket to London. A night train went from Amsterdam to the coast where the train was loaded on a ferry, crossed the English Channel, was off loaded and went directly into London. Once on the train I did not have to get off until it arrived in London, so it was a great way to cross the channel and sleep at the same time. Once I had my ticket in hand it was off to one last day of playing tourist. It was time to see Amsterdam.

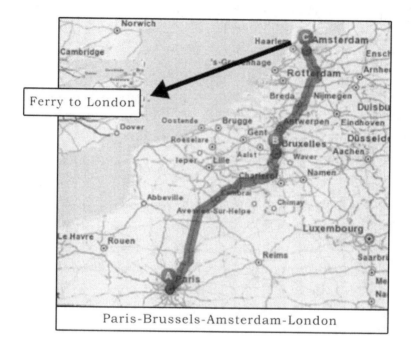

Paris-Brussels-Amsterdam-London

At the Dam

"Crazy scene isn't it?" said the guy next to me as he lit up a joint. I had my crossing to England booked and had enjoyed my last full day in Europe. Amsterdam's unique architecture and cosmopolitan culture, the Anne Frank House, and a nice sunny day had already made the day memorable by the time I sat down in Amsterdam's Dam Square in the early afternoon. I had to be at the train station by 5:00 PM and was finishing the day watching people.

Like every big city I had visited in Europe - London, Copenhagen, Hannover, Heidelberg, Paris, and Brussels - Amsterdam had a central gathering spot for young people to hang out. Dam Square was arguably the wildest, most open, most diverse, and most international of any of the city centers I had visited. Here young people could congregate, share their ideas and drugs, or just be seen.

Amsterdam always had a reputation for being a liberal, open minded city in regards to drugs, alcohol, and sexual interests. It clearly had the most cosmopolitan culture of any city I had visited. Rich and poor, businessmen, merchants, housewives, and working class walked down the same streets. Blond, blue eyed Dutch sat together with Eastern Europeans, Africans and Asians. Heterosexuals, homosexuals, drugs, booze, and just about anything else you could think was right there at The Dam.

The young man next to me seemed to fit the stereotype of the youth counter-culture. He was of mixed race, with long, scraggly hair, an unshaven face, a dirty shirt and holey blue jeans. But he also exuded a sense of confidence and intelligence.

"So you're an American." He correctly observed. "Where you from?"

"Yep, I'm from Michigan. Today's my last day before heading home tomorrow. What about you?" I had learned to be curious of other travelers and to extend conversations their way.

"Me - I'm a Brit. Actually, I'm on holiday from Oxford. How long you been in Europe?"

"Thirty days, but they have gone by fast. I've gone from London, north through England to Edinburgh, then by ferry to Norway and train to Sweden. In Sweden I stayed with a friend for about four days, then went through Copenhagen, south through Germany to Heidelberg, then Paris, Brussels, and here. It's been a whirlwind trip, but it was all the time I could manage."

"Why the rush man?" the Brit asked.

"Well - I have got to get back to college, but I'll tell you, I've had a crazy summer. I started traveling at the end of May - hitchhiked out to San Francisco, then up to the Pacific coast to the Seattle, Washington area, did six weeks of army boot camp, then came over to Europe. I've probably traveled 10,000 miles this summer. It's been great - I've seen so much and met so many fantastic people. But, to be honest, I'm ready to go home and get back into a more established routine. So, what's your deal?" I asked. "You said you're from Oxford. That's pretty impressive. What you doing here?"

He laughed and offered me a toke on his joint. I obliged.

"You seemed surprised when I said I was from Oxford. Don't fit your expectations? Actually, I'm working on my PhD in sociology. My long hair and clothes help me fit in, so people will talk to me and help my research. You probably thought I was just another druggie from Amsterdam - just another hippie in the square. Well, that's okay - most people here just want to be seen and want to communicate with a friend. Their appearance is just something that goes with the scene, ya know?"

"Oh - I admit I was a little surprised," I confessed, "but I shouldn't have been. I've met so many cool people this summer, both here and in the States that I should know better than to judge someone by their appearance."

My scholarly friend said, "It's hard to get past the appearances. We all do it. That's how I knew you were an American. Its part of the game we play when we look at people. It's especially true here. These kids want to be seen. Most of these people want us to think they are free. They want to talk about their individuality, their independence, and free love and all that shit. But the reality is, they need someone to share their time with and to BS with just as much as anyone. Look around. Nobody is really by themselves. They come here to this mob scene so they can find someone to share their thoughts with. Even if it's just splitting a joint, or getting high together, these free spirits need companionship just as much as anyone does."

He was right. I looked around and noticed that no one was alone – they all had someone they were talking to.

He continued. "That's definitely true with the group you're looking at right now. One thing I've learned in my studies is that most of these so called hippies are just rebellious youth trying to figure out what they want to do and where they want to go with their life. Lots of them already have good jobs lined up and are using this time to express what they believe is their last opportunity for freedom in their lives. Many will be professional businessmen, accountants, doctors or lawyers soon with short hair, a three piece suit, wives and families and all the other things we associate with the establishment. They just have not decided they want to give up this life of independence and rebellion."

As he said that, a well-dressed older couple walked by, looked at the crowd and gave a disapproving shake of their heads. I wondered what was going through their minds.

"Every generation rebels against their elders to some extent. It's just that this generation of Baby Boomers is so big, has so much offered to it, and is so visible on TV, that it seems so much more rebellious than other groups before it."

"I can see that," I said in agreement. "My grand-mother rebelled against the accepted order by home-steading and raising her family as a single mother. My own mother talks about how she was criticized for swooning over Frank Sinatra in the 1940's. So I guess it's only natural our generation should make news by being rebels, too."

My British scholar added "Many of these kids don't really have it figured out. They don't know what they want to do. That's the part that is unfortunate. They will hang around, be dependent on society to protect and provide for them, and will eventually end up in some dead end position. It's tough to figure out how best we can help them."

I thought about what he said for a minute. "You know, I really appreciate this talk. I was just thinking about what I had learned this summer, and you've hit on the most significant result of this whole summer of traveling, seeing places, and meeting people."

"Why do you say that? What are you thinking? Maybe I'll have to add you to my research." He said with a sly smile.

I took one more look around at the crowd of youth and gathered my thoughts.

"Well - back in May, when I started hitchhiking west, I was searching for something. I didn't know what it was, but I needed some answers. I was trying to be a little rebellious in my own way. Sure, I wasn't a hippie, didn't have long hair or any radical ideas, and yeah, I came from a nice, white, middle class family - but I was unsure about what I was going to do in the future and where I was going in my personal life. So, maybe I fit into this group more than I want to admit. I've seen and learned a lot this summer. I've seen some spectacular scenery, experienced interesting events, and met a lot of different people. They have all had their own perspective on life, politics, and society. I've tried to listen to what they had to say, and in the process, I've gained a much broader perspective of who I am, and what I want to do with my life."

"Well - good. Go on, man."

My mind was racing now, because I could see where I wanted to go. "I want to teach school. I need to go back and finish my senior year with good grades, and then I'll do my military service, get out and start teaching. I think I have a lot of things I can offer kids. I want to get married, have a family, and live the good middle class life. I've played around with the counter-culture thing - the freedom, the independence, the solo traveling - and it isn't for me. I need a more organized, settled life. It may take me some time to get there, but I think I've learned that's what I want."

"Sounds good man. It really does. It sounds like it was a great summer for you in many ways."

"Yeah - and you helped me sum it up, just by listening and talking to me. Thanks."

"My pleasure. Glad I could help. Now don't miss that train and ferry." With that, he got up and moved to the other side of the square.

On the last day of my long summer of independence and freedom, I came to the conclusion I had not been truly independent, or alone, on this adventure. My fondest memories were of the times when I was with others. Whether it was with the unnamed drivers I rode with in the states, the new friends like Art Kennedy or Mick or Brian or Herr Winckler, or even the fellow travelers who would share a story or some advice about the next city, I was rarely alone or independent. I needed, and often sought, companionship. People can think they are alone in this world, but we are a social animal and need partners to have a complete life.

I spent the rest of the afternoon watching the circus around me and thinking of all the wonderful people and places I had experienced. My summer adventure was nearing an end and this was the perfect time to reflect on what I had experienced since May. Soon it was time for the last leg of my trip.

An Unexpected Party

The next night, September 1, 1971, I was at Gatwick Airport south of London waiting for my flight back to the United States. I had boarded the train in Amsterdam and ferried across the English Channel without incident, so I was feeling good about getting home on time. After more than three months on the road, sleeping in hostels, parks, and train stations, and eating junk food, I was ready for a comfortable bed, good food, and family. I had enjoyed my adventure, but now it was time to get back to normal - whatever that was. I was crammed into a small international waiting area with over 200 people awaiting our plane and overnight flight to New York City, then on to Detroit.

Our departure time came and went with no plane at the terminal. Soon, we were over two hours late and there had not been any explanation. Worse yet, there was no one from the airline to give us an idea when we would leave. It seemed like a repeat of the events in Detroit. It was very warm and uncomfortable in the crowded waiting area, so it did not take long before there were complaints and demands for something to be done.

Finally, about 9:00 p.m. - three hours after the scheduled departure time - a couple of men from the airline appeared and announced our flight would not be departing that night and we were all being rebooked on a flight leaving the next morning. The hot, impatient, upset crowd put out a collective howl of protest. After some frantic phone calls, the airline agreed to bus us to a hotel, buy us a meal, and bring us back in the morning for the next flight.

The last night turned into a party. Most of the passengers were young college students returning home after summer excursions in Europe. I discovered no one had experienced Europe quite like I did. Many of them had been on guided tours or stayed in one country on an overseas study program. But nobody else had traveled through ten countries in twenty-eight days, climbed mountains, played rugby, visited schools, had wine in a 300 year old house, or slept in train stations, parks, and even garages in an attempt to see as much of Europe as possible.

I met a student from Purdue University named Randy while waiting at Gatwick, so we decided to room together. Most of the passengers, including Randy and myself, figured we would sleep on the plane tomorrow. Since we now had one more night in Europe – and it was being paid for by the airline - we would make the most of it.

We arranged our seating for dinner at the same table as two young ladies, Kelly and Susan. Kelly soon went to meet some other friends after dinner, but

Susan - a tall, shapely, very flirtatious blond - seemed enamored with the conversation and wine both Randy and I were liberally giving her. After a filling meal with a couple bottles of wine, we went into the hotel bar and continued to party. There were lots of stories to tell about where we had been and what we had experienced. As the night went on - and the liquor continued to flow - many of those adventures became more fantasy than reality.

Finally, about 4:00 in the morning I drunkenly made my way to our room. The night was not over though. Upon stumbling into the room, I discovered Randy and Susan had arrived before me. They were sitting on the bed - fully clothed - laughing and sharing another bottle of wine. I am not sure how long they had been there, but I think my presence made Susan more comfortable.

"Hey, now we're all here!" she laughed. "Come on Tom, hop up here and have another drink!"

Randy looked a little disappointed, but laughed anyway and sarcastically added, "Yeah! What the Hell! We've been together all night. What are a couple more hours?"

We thought we would just stay up the rest of the night, but after another bottle of wine, some very exaggerated stories, and juvenile attempts at sexual advances, it did not happen. As might be seen in a bad comedy, we were all too drunk to do anything and eventually passed out on the bed, fully clothed.

Before we knew it our 7:00 a.m. wake-up call came. We looked around a little sheepishly and giggled like little kids when we tried to remember what happened. Susan innocently kissed both Randy and me on the cheek; we got up, and prepared to go to the airport. After a summer of trying to sleep with a girl, I had finally succeeded, but did not even remember what happened! All I had to show for the night together was an address - which I lost - and a bad hangover.

Thank goodness nothing else happened to delay the trip home. We got on the bus, got to the airport, and took off. I arrived back in Detroit on the evening of September 2, 1971. My parents and Jackie were there to meet me. Jackie looked even better than she had in July, confirming my plans to marry her. My fantastic summer adventure of growth and discovery was over, but the rest of my life was just beginning.

My last journal entry was made somewhere over the Atlantic on my way home.

September 2:

9:00 PM – Finally going home!

"Respect, love and friendship are shown most clearly by words and acts in everyday contacts. A stranger in a

strange land remains forever an alien, unless he returns as much as he takes."

From: <u>Be At Home in Europe</u> by Simon, from the "Pan Am Clipper"

I'm not sure how to sum all this up after forty years. It was a remarkable trip and it still impacts my thoughts and feelings. Maybe the best summary was written soon after I got to San Francisco and was sitting in the comfort of Aunt Becky's house. I wrote a letter to Jackie which said:

"I had some wonderful experiences coming out here. I met some very interesting people and had some good rides... I got rides with truck drivers, salesmen, kids, cowboys, marines, farmers, and even two dizzy, ugly girls. A kid in Wyoming let me stay overnight with him out of the rain, a truck driver bought me dinner and a guy went five miles out of his way so I could see Fort Laramie, Wyo. I saw Chicago, Salt Lake City, Oshkosh, Neb. mountains, prairies, hills, farms, rivers, lakes, oceans, sunshine, clouds, hot and cold, and rain. And I saw God! The whole thing was great and undiscribable [sic]".

So Why Did I Do It?

"So why do we do it?
What good is it?
Does it teach you anything?
Like determination? Invention?
Improvisation?
Foresight? Hindsight?
Love?
Art? Music? Religion?
Strength or patience or accuracy or quickness
or tolerance or
Which wood will burn and how long is a day and how far
is a mile
And how delicious is watery and smokey green pea soup
And how to rely
On your
Self?"

From <u>On the Loose</u>, by Terry and Renny Russell

Yes, it was a time of transition. The world was changing. Baby Boomers were getting positions of leadership. Europe was recovering from World War II and would soon be united. Communism would soon fade as a threat to the Free World. And I was changing.

I had found what I was searching for. I had developed my religious beliefs, become more environmentally conscious, and accepted different lifestyles and cultures. I had formed opinions I would carry through life concerning politics, international events, and America's role in the world. I had learned who I was, what I wanted, and where I was going. I had experienced freedom, independence, and learned I needed relationships and organization.

The summer adventure was over and I was home. The questions started when the trip ended. Why DID I do it? What DID I gain? Was it worth the sleepless nights, the endless hassle of waiting for rides or trying to catch a train? Was it worth standing in the heat, cold, rain, and dust to try to get somewhere for just a fleeting moment? What DID I learn through it all? Deep inside myself I could answer those questions, but even forty years later it is hard to explain to others. I did learn to rely on myself. I matured and gained experience dealing with different situations. I looked at the world with different expectations. I was no longer the innocent young man who started the trip.

The summer of '71 gave me a new sense of purpose. I went back to school with a new vigor, a new confidence, and a new outlook. History classes were more relevant and English classes more significant. My love life took on a different tone as I realized Jackie was the woman I wanted to marry. I procrastinated asking her until the following spring, and in my new traveling style I proposed on a Spring Break trip while camping at

Mammoth Cave National Park. It seems a little corny now, but at the time, it was right.

After graduation in May, 1972, I was commissioned a Second Lieutenant in the U.S. Army, married Jackie in August, and received orders for Germany. So, less than eighteen months after hitchhiking around Germany, Jackie and I were back in country living in Karlsruhe just down the autobahn from Heidelberg and Speyer. This time we were living in a comfortable apartment and driving a new Audi, so it was much more civilized than my first experience.

We lived in Germany three years, and since then I have returned to Europe numerous times - as an army reservist, with my family (at which time I kept my vow to return to Paris and enjoy an expensive glass of wine on the Champs Elysees,) and as a chaperone for student tours. I have traveled to the western United States many times and continue to be impressed with the beauty of the plains, the mountains, and the wide open spaces. But I have never had the human experiences, or learned so much about people, culture, and society, as I did in the period from May to August 1971.

It was the people I met who made the summer memorable and more than just a tourist trip through the United States and Europe. Over fifty drivers had enough trust in humanity, and empathy for a young man, to pick up a stranger and help him along his way. These people shared ideas, listened, laughed, and offered advice. Some shared food and drink. Some bought me meals, and a special group offered me food, shelter, and rest when I needed it most. Throughout the summer I met people who reaffirmed my faith in the goodness of humanity. These people demonstrated understanding, patience, hope, and charity towards the world around them. They were not only nice to me, but it seemed an innate part of their character to be hopeful and caring to everyone they met. This demonstrated love is what made the summer special.

Much has changed in the forty plus years since the summer of '71. History will record political events such as Watergate, the end of the Vietnam War, the fall of Communism, the unification of Germany, the develop-ment of the European Union, terrorist attacks, and wars in the Middle East and Afghanistan. Cultural and social changes have occurred too, with the growth of technology, improved communications, and better transportation. But many of the problems of 1971 are still issues in today's world. Diversity and immigration, America's global presence, war, the environment, political partisanship, and family values are still topics of discussion among America's leaders and the public.

The early Seventies were a time of anti-war protests and throughout the summer I heard many arguments for and against our involvement in Vietnam. From those protests we learned it is okay to question the government and to openly express our opinions. Op-posing a governmental policy is not un-American. In fact, it is one of the privileges that make America great. Being a good American demands that we expect openness and honesty from our leaders. The discussions and exchange of ideas allowed me to clarify my own thoughts on the Vietnam War. Even today we need to be able to listen to both sides of political debate and be accepting to all ideas and opinions.

My travel adventures taught me not to judge people by their appearances. I often wonder if I would have experienced the same treatment if I was not a white, short haired, clean dressed, obviously middle class, innocent young man. If I had long hair, a scraggly beard, and dirty clothes would I have been as welcome in peoples' homes? If I had been African American, Hispanic, or Asian would I have been picked up as often and shared the same experiences? Probably not. I like to think Americans see past skin color or ethnic background when demonstrating their kindness to others, but reality frequently proves otherwise.

The United States brags about its diversity and being the Melting Pot of the World, but it is still a nation where race and ethnicity create a tremendous difference in life experiences. We are a nation of immigrants, yet we have extreme prejudices towards them. Immigrants helped build this nation, fighting in our wars, powering the industrial growth, settling new lands, and adding intellectual knowledge. We want the world to see us as open minded and accepting, yet we cannot practice those characteristics at home. It should be possible for anyone, of any racial or ethnic background, to enjoy the dreams and experiences I had.

So Why Did I Do It?

I had many discussions about the Vietnam War and America's international presence. These discussions forced me to think more about foreign affairs. My travels, especially the European phase of the summer, made me more aware of America's image abroad and helped form my opinions concerning overseas policy. I became much more international in my outlook. I realized how America's actions affected Europe - not just politically, but also economically, socially, and culturally. Conversely, European policies made an impact on the United States. Americans need to be aware of how our actions, both personal and as a nation, look to the other peoples of the world. Many Americans, like the ugly American who insisted the British did not know how to cook roast beef, tend to think the American way is the only way. That attitude will not work in the twenty-first century.

Events and experiences on my trip - such as the week in Europe of no money due to the political and economic policy changes in the U.S. - taught me how interconnected economic and political issues are. That is even truer today. Today's global marketplace has caused many changes in our lives and culture. Political decisions are influenced by our dependence on other nations' labor force and products. It has impacted our job opportunities. In the 1960's and 1970's a young person could get a job with little more than a high school diploma, work on the factory assembly line for a good wage and benefits, and retire with a good pension. That is much more difficult today. Those jobs have been replaced by robotics and cheaper overseas labor.

Regardless of what politicians may promise or people may hope, those jobs are not going to come back. That is the reality of globalization.

Probably the biggest changes on economics in the last forty years are the improvements in technology and communications. Today business and trade is globalized beyond anything that could be dreamed of forty years ago. America's economy is now dependent on international events. Whether there is an earthquake in Japan, war in the Middle East, or a financial crisis in Europe, our economy will be affected. Business and industry hinge on the success or failures of the global market. American businesses sell more and more products in Asia, India, and Africa, and take advantage of the cheaper labor available in those areas. Better transportation and communications make it possible to produce products overseas and still get them to the United States cheaper than if they were made here. These are some of the basic principles of a capitalistic system - to take advantage of the greatest market possible, and to produce the product as cheaply as possible. This has had a huge impact on America's economy as jobs and money have moved overseas. We need to update our industrial and manufacturing sectors - and in the meantime take care of the older workers who lost their jobs due to this change.

As I watched students in Heidelberg sell their blue jeans and American sweatshirts to black marketers, I realized sooner or later trade and culture would bring the world closer together, which will result in a world of more understanding and cooperation. The communist world of Eastern Europe and the Soviet Union collapsed in large part because they could not prevent their citizens from seeing, and wanting, the clothes, automobiles, music, foods, and freedoms of the capitalistic world. Just as the world came closer together because of "Levis, Coke, and Rock and Roll" in the Seventies and Eighties, so the peoples of Asia, India, and Africa desire the freedoms and individualism of the democratic world. Today the Middle East is in turmoil and changing as a result of the communications revolution. Their citizens are learning about democracy and freedom via the internet and social media and are demanding changes in their government. This is happening because of the global marketplace and business world. The process may seem slow, but it is happening.

My summer experience taught me a greater acceptance of personal freedoms and choices. Throughout the journey I made choices that shaped me - not only the immediate success or failure of the trip, but also decisions affecting my future life. Decisions had to be made quickly and intelligently. Should I take a particular route, ride with a certain person, or be open or private? I learned to accept differences in people. I met rich, poor, drug users, homosexuals, hippies, conservatives, liberals, pro and anti-war, city slickers, farmers, Christians, Muslims, and Jews. They all had something to offer the world, and they had the right to choose the life they were living. I may not have agreed with their choices, but I respected their right to live that life. Religion, sexual orientation, and lifestyle are personal choices. Governments should not try to mandate or regulate private decisions such as these. The right and freedom to live our life our way is important and should not be infringed upon.

Today's technological advancements make the problems I experienced in 1971 laughable. If I were to make the same trip today, it would be much different. I would not wonder where I was staying, since I could use the internet to book a room in a hostel or cheap hotel well in advance. I could call ahead and notify my friends of arrival times, and I could email my parents or Jackie when I was feeling homesick. Train and ferry schedules could be accessed weeks in advance for improved planning. Of course things would be a bit more expensive, but having a stable Euro and not changing currency at every border would make things much easier.

The beautiful landscapes of the American west and the rivers and hills of central Europe stood out in contrast to the industrial might and success of the steel mills, mining, oil refineries, and manufacturing plants passed along the way. Both were indicative of the power of people to shape the world. But the environment and the natural forces cannot be ignored in order to produce more profit. We must guard the delicate balance of nature. While the scientific proof of global warming may still be questionable, there can be no argument humans have caused extreme environmental damage over the years. Whether it is global warming, toxic waste, or over production without concern for the resources, we must take care not to overdo it. It is easy to ignore environmental concerns and regulations in the name of providing more jobs and making a greater profit. We can pump more oil, cut down more trees, pollute the waters with run-off and declare the next generation will fix it. We can do all of this in the name of job creation and profits. We have put things off too long - we need to change and address environmental problems.

Just as our politics and economy need to become more global, we also need to develop a more global attitude toward religious differences. Traveling taught me to appreciate the cultural and religious ideas of the world. The beauty of a Mormon temple, a Catholic cathedral, or a Muslim mosque demonstrate not only the architectural ingenuity of society, but also the religious devotion of the people who built them. Every day the religious ideas of Christians, Muslims, Jews, Hindus, and Buddhists come into contact with each other. If we are going to have a global world we must appreciate the religious ideals of the various people with whom we are going to trade. Just as we have a nation built on the diversity of races, creeds, and ideas, we must also be a nation that accepts the religious diversity of its people. We are not - and never have been - strictly a Christian nation, excluding all other religions. If we want peace, morality, and goodness, then an acceptance and understanding of all religions will make it easier to achieve that goal.

My conversations with Europeans showed me how much other nations look to the United States as a model for freedom and social change. Hopefully we, in turn, can look at their contributions and learn from them. For example, most European nations have some sort of national health care program. Some work and some do not, but when the U.S. government discusses health care we should take the ideas that work in Europe and around the world and institute them here. We do not have to invent something just to say it is the American way. We can learn from what they have done before us.

In 1977, after five years in the army, I settled into civilian life. We had two wonderful sons. I taught history, coached basketball and cross country, and served eighteen more years in the Army Reserves. I taught high school history for thirty-three years, but always remembered my experiences while working with students. The summer of 1971 gave me an insight into people's thinking that proved helpful while teaching. I could talk about America's growth and history from a personal perspective. When teaching European history students respected my experience and enjoyed my stories of living and traveling in Europe.

After teaching history I realize the fallacy of trying to relive it, or "going back to the good old days." History is a guide, not a rulebook. History shows us the mistakes and the successes of the past and gives us guidance for the future. When we study history, we realize things are always changing - life does not and cannot stay the same. History teaches us that progress and change are good. They have made our world exciting. The circumstances in 1971 were right for me to successfully complete the trip with no serious complications or mishaps. However, those circumstances will never be the same again and I can never relive that summer - except in my mind. History teaches to keep moving forward and to have an open mind toward events. We cannot go back - only forward.

These experiences will stay with me forever. The changes in our society and culture since then are significant, but the basic values of America - freedom, independence, democracy, free thought - have not changed. Europe has gone through tremendous change with the collapse of communism and the development of the European Union, but the openness, kindness, and hopefulness of its people are still important aspects of their daily lives.

When I returned home and talked to friends and family I found it hard to describe the significance of my trip. I could talk about the typical tourist spots - the Rockies, Golden Gate, London, Paris, and Amsterdam, and all the other famous places. But those things did not come close to getting to the real impact of my experiences. It was hard to describe the impact of being in the rain to watch the sunrise, or standing in one small town for seven hours, or to be trusted by people you have just met to share a meal and a place to sleep, or the myriad of other experiences of the summer. Certain things in life cannot be fully explained, even forty years later.

In his song *Rocky Mountain High*, John Denver says, "He was born in the summer of his twenty-second year, coming home to a place he'd never been before. Left yesterday behind him, might say he was born again." Every time I hear that song I feel a personal connection. It was my twenty-second year. I did leave my old life behind. And I was born again.

So would I ever do it again? Could I ever do it again? I do not think so. Since 1971 Jackie and I have traveled extensively throughout Europe and the United States, and we have more places we want to see. But I could never recreate that summer - nor do I want to. I happened to be in the right place at the right time. Was I lucky? Definitely. I do not even want to think of the things that could have happened during that three month odyssey. But most of all, when thinking about the summer of '71, I remember the love and faith extended to me by my parents. Now that I'm a parent myself I can't believe they let me go - even gave their blessing for the trip. I realize what a difficult decision it was and how many times they must have wondered where I was and what I was doing. At the time I knew it was special, but as the years go by, I appreciate even more how special their decision was. And, of course, how special they were.

And, I'm sorry Dad - it did not stop my wanderlust.

About the Author

Tom Laughlin is a retired high school history teacher and coach living in Grand Haven, Michigan. He taught American and European History and coached varsity cross country and eighth grade basketball for over thirty years. He is also a retired Lieutenant Colonel after twenty three years of active and reserve duty in the army.

He and his wife Jackie have two sons who are married, with two beautiful grandchildren each. Jackie and Tom still enjoy traveling through life together.